IN JAPAN

Philip Hinder

Language consultants

Nobuo Suzuki
Tetsushi Sato
Hiroko Tsuchiya

EMC Publishing

About *In Japan*

In Japan is a quick, easy and entertaining introduction to the language, land and people of Japan. It is written by a **gaijin** (foreigner) who lives in Japan, helped by English-speaking Japanese people, who are used to helping foreigners over the initial language and cultural barriers. Only by beginning to understand the language can students appreciate the full fascination of the country. *In Japan* makes this possible by introducing the language with topics such as Japanese food, traveling in and out of Tokyo, ancient festivals, modern industry, entertainment, shopping, history and the regions of Japan.

To make reading Japanese simple, romanized Japanese words are usually shown in **bold type**. The meaning of the word or phrase follows in brackets, if it cannot be guessed easily from the context or the picture. Many pages of the book have a special Japanese language section, headed with the Japanese characters 日本語. These mean **Nihongo**, the Japanese language. In the **Nihongo** sections, Japanese words are given in **rōmaji** (romanized script) and also in the Japanese scripts, **hiragana** or **katakana**, plus a few **kanji**. The different scripts are explained on pages 8–9.

In Japan helps students speak some Japanese from the very start. Speaking practise activities begin with 口, the character which means **kuchi**, or mouth. There are two kinds of question activities: those with numbers in squares (for example 1) can be answered by looking at the photographs and illustrations, or reading the text on the page. Answers are on page 80. Questions marked with letters in circles (for example Ⓐ) have no set answers. Why not discuss them with other students?

In Japan is ideal for students of the Japanese language, the land and people. It also provides an essential preparation for visitors who want to understand what they see in Japan.

Designer: Wendi Watson
Editor: Picot Cassidy
Illustrators: Alan Suttie, Cedric Knight
Cartoonist: David Lock

© Chancerel 1992
PN 5 4 3 /97 96 95

ISBN 0-8219-0921-5
Catalog no. 58252

Published by:
EMC Publishing
300 York Avenue
Saint Paul
Minnesota 55101, USA

Printed in Hong Kong

Contents

Welcome to Japan

Japan lies off the mainland of East Asia. It has four main islands: **Honshū**, **Hokkaidō**, **Kyūshū** and **Shikoku**. In addition, there are nearly 4,000 tiny islands, mostly uninhabitated. Seventy percent of Japan's land area of 377,435 square kilometers (145,727 square miles) is mountainous.

*There are about 123 million people in Japan. Many people live in such cities as **Tōkyō**, **Ōsaka** and **Nagoya**. Japanese people have the world's highest life expectancy: 75.91 years for men and 81.77 years for women.*

*Although the writing system, consisting of borrowed Chinese **kanji** (characters) and two other groups of symbols, **hiragana** and **katakana**, may seem difficult, the spoken language is surprisingly straightforward and pronunciation is fairly simple.*

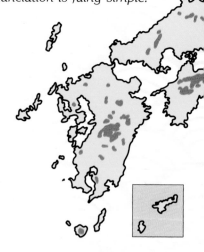

Land under 1,000 m (3,000 ft)	Land over 1,000 m (3,000 ft)

*Snow-covered **Fuji-san** (Mount **Fuji**), which rises to 3,776 meters (12,388 feet), is Japan's highest mountain. For centuries, it has been considered sacred and its 'perfect' cone shape has provided inspiration for many poets and artists.*

(A) Do you know the names of any places in Japan? What do you know about these places?

*The flag represents the sun. Japan is known in Japanese as **Nihon** which means 'the origin of the sun.'*

N

Akihito became emperor in 1989 following the death of his father, **Hirohito**, who ruled for 63 years.

The emperor was once thought of as a 'living god,' but his role is now that of head of state for ceremonial and diplomatic activities.

B What Japanese people have you heard of? What are they famous for?

Japan has the largest trade surplus in the world, even though it has to buy from abroad nearly all its oil and timber and the other raw materials which it lacks. Its success is due to the high-quality products which it sells to other countries. Unemployment is low and stands at about 2.5 percent of the working population.

Teenagers listen to Japanese and foreign pop and rock music. Groups, with some musicians as young as 13, can be seen performing on Sundays in **Yoyogi** Park in **Tōkyō**. They hope to impress a talent scout and be signed up for a television appearance.

Speaking Japanese

Nihongo

Nihongo is the Japanese language. Each region has its own dialect, but a standard version of Japanese is taught in schools and understood by people all over Japan. This 'standard' Japanese is based on the dialect from the **Tōkyō** area.

To show respect for older people, younger Japanese ▶ *use a polite form of Japanese.*

Pronouncing Japanese

When you speak Japanese, it is important to make each syllable the same length and to say it clearly.

Vowels:
- Vowel sounds are shorter than their English equivalents:

  a as in *rather*   **e** as in *get*
  i as in *beat*   **o** as in *hot*
  u as in *book*

- When **i** and **u** follow a consonant, they are not always sounded clearly. For example, **desu** sounds like *dess*, **shita** like *shta*, and **suki** like *sski*.

- Two vowels together should be pronounced as separate sounds and not combined. For example, **kōen** (park) is pronounced *koh en*.

- Some syllables can be combined to form one. For example, **kya** is a combination of **ki** and **ya**, and **chu** is a combination of **chi** and **yu**.

- In this book, if you see a line above a vowel, it means that the vowel is twice as long as usual, as in **Tōkyō** (*toh kyoh*).
  The vowel **i** is the only exception to this. The longer **i** sound is shown as **ii**.

Consonants
- The pronunciation of consonants is not as strong as English. **R** is halfway between an *r* and an *l* sound. **V** is pronounced the same as **b**.

- If there is a double consonant, pause slightly before saying the consonant. For example, try saying **kekkō** (all right).

日本語

Nihongo o hanashite kudasai.

Nihongo ga sukoshi dekimasu.
I can speak a little Japanese.

Wakarimasu ka?
Do you understand?

Hai. Wakarimasu.   **Iie. Wakarimasen.**
Yes. I understand.   No. I don't understand.

Bicycle wa nihongo de nan to iimasu ka?
How do you say *bicycle* in Japanese?

If you want someone to repeat what they have said, say:

Mō ichido itte kudasai.

☐ Please speak some Japanese. Here are some phrases to practise.

Ohayō gozaimasu	Good morning.
Konnichiwa	Hello.
Konbanwa	Good evening.
Dōmo arigatō	Thank you.
Sayonara	Goodbye.

Gairaigo

In Japanese, thousands of **gairaigo** (foreign words) have been 'borrowed' from other languages, sometimes because there was no suitable Japanese word. **Gairaigo** come from French, German, Dutch and Portuguese, but especially from English.

The sound of borrowed words has to be changed to fit with Japanese pronunciation. In most cases, consonants must be followed by a vowel, for example 'hot dog' would be **hotto doggu**. In addition, there is no difference in the way Japanese people pronounce certain pairs of letters: *L* and *R*, and *B* and *V*. All of this has led to a new 'language' called Japlish, in which **gairaigo** are either used with the same meaning as in the original language, or take on a special Japanese meaning.

☐ Look at the list of **gairaigo** below. Practice reading them aloud.

a	**kōhii**	coffee
b	**chiizu**	cheese
c	**sandoitchi**	sandwich
d	**poppusu**	pop music
e	**biniiru**	plastic bag
	(from *vinyl*)	
f	**sunakku**	bar
	(from *snack*)	
g	**supiido-ōbā**	speeding
	(from *speed over*)	

*The Japanese word for 'bread' is **pan**. It is taken from Portuguese, because the first bread that the Japanese saw was brought by the Portuguese in the 16th century.*

*Gairaigo that are too long or too difficult to say are shortened. **Wāpuro** is short for word processor and **raji kase** is a radio-cassette recorder.*

*For Japanese people the 'Japlish' expression **sarariiman** ('salary man') describes perfectly the typical employee who works for one company all his life.*

◄ *It has become fashionable among young people and in advertising to use **gairaigo**, even when there is a Japanese word that can be used. People will ask for **miruku** (milk) instead of using **gyū nyū**, the Japanese word.*

☐ Say the following **gairaigo** aloud. Try to work out what they mean.

  a Furaido chikin
  b Jūsu
  c Chokorēto
  d Bebii kā
  e Koin randorii

f *Depāto*

g *Manshon*

Writing Japanese

Hiragana to katakana

All Japanese words can be written in **hiragana**, a writing system with 47 symbols. Each symbol represents a syllable: for example, **ka, ki, ku, ke, ko** or **sa, shi, su, se, so**. On page 78 you can see a chart of all the **hiragana** and how they are written.

Foreign words are usually, but not always, written in **katakana**, which also has 47 symbols. There is a chart on page 79. Both **hiragana** and **katakana** are simplified forms of **kanji** or characters (see page 9.)

Together these writing systems are known as **kana** and it is useful to be able to recognize both. Shops often write the names of goods in **hiragana** instead of the more complicated-looking **kanji**. Menus in western-style cafés and restaurants are mostly written in **katakana**.

*A menu for a hamburger restaurant in **katakana**. The first item for 180 yen is **aisu kōhii** or iced coffee.*

日本語

---

1 Using the **hiragana** chart on page 78, work out what these two Japanese people are called.

        A **B**

かつひろ   よしえ

2 These phrases are in **hiragana**. Write them out in **rōmaji**.

  a どうもありがとう。
  b おはようございます。
  c にほんごをはなしてください。

3 What is the English meaning of each? (See page 6.)

Foreign names are written in **katakana**:

ローズビトラ
Rose Vitola

4 Using the **katakana** chart on page 79, work out who these well-known people are.

  a メルギブソン
  b マドンナ
  c ジョージブッシュ
  d ミハイルゴルバチョフ

(A) How would you write your name in Japanese?

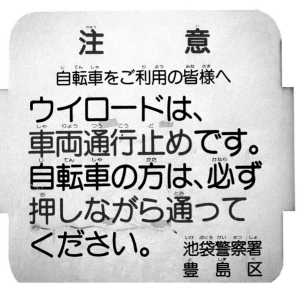

In Japanese, the most important words are written in **kanji**, and the grammatical endings in **hiragana**.

This sign tells people that bicycles must be pushed, not ridden. Above the **kanji** is a **hiragana** equivalent which shows how to pronounce the **kanji**.

*In both **hiragana** and **katakana**, the sounds of k, s, t and h are changed by adding special marks called ˚ (dakuten). K becomes g, s becomes z, t becomes d and h becomes b. Han dakuten ˚ added to h make it into a p sound. See pages 78–79 for a full list of these.*

*In this sign the **hiragana** for ka—か— becomes **ga** when you add **dakuten**— が.*

おがわまち
Ogawamachi

When Japanese words are written with Roman letters, these are called **rōmaji**. This road sign is written in **kanji** and **rōmaji**.

Kanji

Kanji are characters or symbols that were borrowed from the Chinese about two thousand years ago, because the Japanese had no writing system of their own.

Even today, Chinese and Japanese people can often understand the same **kanji** when it is written, but they cannot understand each other when they speak because their languages sound quite different.

Most **kanji** can be read in two or more different ways. Some can be read in over 20 ways, with the meaning depending on which way the **kanji** is read. For example, 白鳥 means 'swan' when pronounced **hakuchō**, but 'white bird' when read as **shiratori**.

Kanji were originally based on simple pictures, mostly taken from nature. These were later standardized. Additional words are formed by combinations of **kanji**.

The **kanji** for **o tearai** (toilet)

To read a newspaper or a magazine it is necessary to know about 2,000 **kanji**. ▶

Original picture	Modern kanji	Meaning
	火	Fire
	手	Hand
	川	River
	田	Rice paddy-field
	木	Tree
	口	Mouth

Making contact

Konnichiwa!

Here are ways of greeting people you know and those you don't.

Two friends who meet by chance:

> Konnichiwa! Genki?

> Hai. Genki desu.

こんにちは。げんき。
Hello! (Are you) well?

はい。げんきです。
Yes. (I'm) fine.

For a polite way to ask how someone is, say **O genki desu ka**?

Two people meeting at a party:

> Watashi wa Hiroshi desu. Anata no namae wa?

> Mamiko desu.

わたしはひろしです。
あなたのなまえは。
I'm Hiroshi. What's your name?

まみこです。
It's Mamiko.

Introducing someone to another person:

> Kawamura-san. Kochira wa Sasaki-san desu.

> Hajimemashite.

> Dōzo yoroshiku.

かわむらさん、こちらはささきさんです。
Mr Kawamura, this is Miss Sasaki.

はじめまして。 How do you do?
どうぞよろしく。 Pleased to meet you.

Add **san** to the end of a person's name when you are referring to them. Never use **san** when you say your own name.

You use **Hajimemashite** and **Dōzo yoroshiku** when you meet someone for the first time.

Two friends saying good night:

> Ja ne.

> O yasuminasai.

じゃね。
See you, then.

おやすみなさい。
Good night.

Ja ne is more informal than **Sayonara**, which is another way of saying goodbye.

Use **O yasuminasai** when you are saying goodbye to someone late at night (before bedtime).

Hajimemashite

Japanese people start bowing from the age of one, prompted by their parents! It is the natural way to greet someone and say goodbye.

There are rules for bowing. If you bow deeply and hold the bow it is a way of showing that the other person has a higher status than you. Younger people and those used to dealing with foreigners will shake hands when meeting people from abroad.

*When people who don't know each other meet ▶ for the first time in formal situations, they bow and exchange **meishi** (name cards).*

◀ *A **meishi** gives a person's name, the name, address and phone number of the company he works for, as well as his department and job. Sometimes there is an English equivalent on the other side. It's polite to show you've read the card before putting it away carefully.*

*The only women who use **meishi** are the few who hold important jobs, or those who work for very small companies and deal directly with clients.*

It's all right to phone someone at work. It is often the best way of getting in touch because working hours are so long that people don't arrive home until late at night.

Sumimasen!

Sumimasen can mean several things: "Excuse me," "I'm sorry" or "Thank you" (for taking the trouble to do something). It is a helpful word to use in many situations.

To avoid embarrassment, look at what others around you are doing. Most Japanese are tolerant of foreigners who don't know Japanese customs, but they do appreciate it if you make an effort to do things the Japanese way.

REMEMBER:
* Take off your shoes before going into someone's house or walking on the **tatami**-mat floor in a restaurant.
* Don't cross the road when the signal for pedestrians is red, even if there are no cars in sight.
* Bring a small gift if you visit someone's house. People often exchange gifts. A small souvenir from your country or a cake shows your gratitude.

1 What would you say in Japanese when:
   a you want to attract a waiter's attention in a café.
   b you want to say good night.
   c you want to ask someone's name.
   d you meet someone for the first time.
   e you want to tell someone your name.
   f you want to say goodbye to a friend.

Regional round-up

Japan's largest island, **Honshū**, consists of five major regions. The other three main islands are **Hokkaidō**, **Kyūshū** and **Shikoku**.

Each region is subdivided into **ken** (prefectures). There are 44 **ken** in all. The islands of **Hokkaidō** and **Okinawa** are not subdivided. Each is both a region and a **ken**.

Chūbu

Main cities: Nagoya, Shizuoka, Gifu, Niigata, Toyama

The Japanese Alps are located in **Chūbu**, the central region. **Nagano-ken** (prefecture) has spectacular scenery. Visitors can go trekking and mountaineering in summer and skiing in winter.

In the north of **Chūbu** on **Nihonkai** (Sea of Japan) is **Kanazawa**, where the people perform traditional **nō** and comedy plays. In the south is **Fuji-san** (Mount **Fuji**) and **Nagoya**, a major city of more than two million inhabitants.

Chūgoku

Main cities: Hiroshima, Okayama, Shimonoseki, Matsue, Tottori

Chūgoku is divided by mountains into **San-yo**, the southern part, and **San-in**, the northern part. **San-yo** has a coast on **Seto Naikai** (the Inland Sea). Old Japan is preserved in **Kurashiki**, with its traditional houses and many museums.

The biggest city, **Hiroshima**, was the first city to be destroyed by an atomic bomb in 1945.

Kansai

Main cities: Ōsaka, Kōbe, Kyōto, Nara

Nara and, later, **Kyōto**, were the ancient capitals of Japan. The temples and gardens of these cities are internationally famous. In modern times, **Ōsaka** plays a major economic role as Japan's second largest industrial zone. The **Kōbe-Ōsaka-Kyōto** area is almost as densely populated as greater **Tōkyō**.

Shikoku

Main cities: Takamatsu, Matsuyama, Tokushima

Shikoku ('four provinces') is the smallest of the four main islands. It is separated from the main island, **Honshū**, by **Seto Naikai**.

Okinawa

Kyūshū

Main cities: Nagasaki, Fukuoka, Kita Kyūshū, Kumamoto, Kagoshima

Kyūshū, the third largest island, lies close to the Asian mainland. The cultures of China and Korea were introduced to Japan by way of northern **Kyūshū**. During 220 years of isolation up to the 1860s, the port of **Nagasaki** provided Japan's only link with the world.

Okinawa

Main city: Naha

About 650 kilometers (400 miles) south of **Kyūshū** is the island of **Okinawa** (with about 60 smaller islands). The culture and language of the Okinawans are different from other parts of Japan, because the island didn't become integrated into Japan until the 19th century.

There has been a strong American presence in **Okinawa** since the end of World War II. The island was returned to Japan in 1972 and its subtropical beaches have made it a popular year-round vacation destination.

Yama やま

Hokkaidō

Main cities: Sapporo, Hakodate

With six million inhabitants on a large island, **Hokkaidō** has few people relative to many other areas in Japan. Approximately 20,000 of them are **Ainu**, a people who have lived on **Hokkaidō** for centuries.

Because it has wide open spaces, **Hokkaidō** is popular with hikers and campers in summer, and skiers during the long winter.

Tōhoku

Main cities: Sendai, Yamagata, Aomori, Akita

Tōhoku, Japan's main rice-producing area, still has a country atmosphere. Attractions include the coast, lakes, mountains and hot spring resorts. Wooden **kokeshi** dolls, lacquerware and pottery are the traditional crafts in **Tōhoku**. Three of the most popular traditional festivals in Japan are held in **Sendai**, **Akita** and **Aomori**.

Kantō

Main cities: Tōkyō, Yokohama, Chiba

The region is named after the **Kantō** plain which stretches from **Taiheiyō** (the Pacific) in the east to the mountains in the west and north. **Tōkyō**, the Japanese capital, is in **Kantō**.

日本語

Anata wa doko kara kimashita ka?

Watashi wa Ōsaka kara kimashita.

あなたはどこから
きましたか。
Where do you come from?

わたしはおおさか
からきました。
I come from **Ōsaka**.

☐ With a partner.
Look at the picture on the left. Ask your partner where he or she comes from.

Ōsutoraria Igirisu Nyū Jiirando Amerika

Now say what town you are from. Try to make the name sound Japanese, even if it sounds a little exaggerated.

Watashi wa Shikago kara kimashita.

13

Planning to go

Pasupōto, kurejitto kādo...

If you are visiting Japan, of course, you'll need a valid **pasupōto** (passport). A visa is also necessary for most visitors. It is best to check with the Japanese Embassy in your country.

It is important to arrange some health insurance. A stay in a hospital or a visit to the dentist could be very expensive.

Taking travelers' checks is convenient. You will probably have to change them at a bank. **Kurejitto kādo** (credit cards) are now accepted at many hotels, restaurants and stores. In smaller shops and restaurants, if you do not have enough cash, make sure they accept **kurejitto kādo**. Even if there are credit card stickers, you may be politely told, "I'm sorry. We've run out of sales slips," or "Your card is not on my list."

*You can use **kurejitto kādo** in this **resutoran** (restaurant).*

◀ *If you want a Japan Rail Pass, you must buy one before you go to Japan. The pass is valid for seven, 14 or 21 days. It can be used on Japan Railways trains, buses and ferries throughout Japan.*

Sūtsu kēsu no naka ni

- If you're likely to be in Japan during **baiu** (the rainy season) and **taifū** (typhoon) time, pack something in your **sūtsu kēsu** (suitcase) to keep out the rain.
- Also make sure you take all the clothes you need. It may be difficult to find clothes and shoes in larger (non-Japanese) sizes.
- If you are planning to stay with, or to visit a Japanese family, make room in your **sūtsu kēsu** for some small, nicely wrapped gifts from your home country.

Ii tenki desu ne?

Tenki (the weather) depends not only on the time of year but also on the region. The mountainous areas of **Honshū** and **Hokkaidō** can be very cool in the middle of summer. In tropical **Okinawa**, the temperature rarely falls below freezing in winter.

Aki (autumn) and **haru** (spring) are the best times to visit Japan. In October and November, the air is brisk and the leaves change into dramatic autumn colors. Late spring (April and May) is also a good time before **baiu** (the rainy season), which lasts from mid-June to mid-July, and the very hot and humid weather in August. September is the time for **taifū** (typhoons). In **fuyu** (winter) January and February can be cold, but generally they are clear and sunny. The **kanji** (character) for each season appears in the top left of the photo.

Haru はる

Natsu なつ

Aki あき

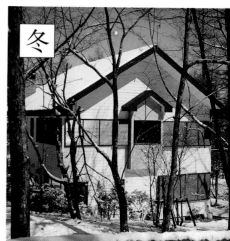

Fuyu ふゆ

--- 日本語 ---

Ii tenki desu ne?
いいてんきですね。
The weather's good, isn't it?

Iya na tenki desu ne?
いやなてんきですね。
The weather's terrible, isn't it?

Samui desu ne?
さむいですね。
It's cold, isn't it?

Suzushii desu ne?
すずしいですね。
It's cool, isn't it?

Atsui desu ne?
あついですね。
It's hot, isn't it?

Mushiatsui desu ne?
むしあついですね。
It's hot and humid, isn't it?

If you agree with what someone is saying about the weather, say:

Sō desu ne.

☐ Look at the pictures on this page. What could you say in Japanese about **tenki** for each one?

15

The sun rises

The origins of Japan

Tens of thousands of years ago Japan was part of the Asian mainland. Land bridges are once thought to have connected Japan to Korea in the south and Siberia in the north. Little is known about the people who lived in Japan before 7000 BC.

Pottery from the **Jōmon** (700–250 BC) and **Yayoi** (250 BC–AD 300) periods has helped archeologists obtain information about early periods in Japanese history. **Jōmon** pottery was discovered in eastern and northern **Honshū**. Reddish-colored **Yayoi** looks something like pottery produced at the same time in South Korea. During the **Yayoi** period developments such as the potter's wheel and the cultivation of rice first appeared.

The first emperor
According to legend, the first emperor of Japan was **Jimmu Tennō**, who was a descendant of the sun goddess **Amaterasu**. In 660 B.C., he made his capital at **Yamato**, which is near present-day **Nara**.

Over the next 400 years, his descendants conquered the tribes of **Honshū** and united them under **Yamato** rule. The foundation of modern Japan dates from the 4th Century AD. Every Japanese emperor claims descent from the early **Yamato** emperors.

Haniwa are pottery figures of people, ▶ *houses and everyday objects. They were discovered in large burial mounds from the* **Kofun** *period (from about 3rd–6th century AD).*

The cultures of China and Korea were an important influence on early Japan. Arts and craft techniques were imported, as well as a writing system from China. Buddhism and Confucianism were introduced and flourished mainly due to the efforts of Prince **Shōtoku** *(574–622).*

──── 日本語 ────

The Japanese call their country **Nihon** or **Nippon** which means literally 'origin of the sun' and is often translated as 'the land of the rising sun'. In **kanji** (characters), **Nihon** is written 日本.

The **kanji** *for 'sun' or 'day' was first drawn as a picture of the sun (far left). Over the years the shape changed until it became the* **kanji** *(left) people use today. It can be read as* **hi, ni, nichi** *or* **ka**.

The **kanji** *for 'origin' developed from a picture of a tree with its roots (far left). The roots represented the idea of origin. The* **kanji** *(left) can be read as* **hon** *or* **moto**.

Hon *also means 'book', because books are regarded as the root of knowledge.*

A Japanese stamp

The Nara Period (AD 710–794)

Up to the **Nara** period, the capital of Japan had changed with the death of each ruler. But the increasing size of the imperial administration made it more difficult to keep moving the capital. In 710, **Heijō-kyō** (now known as **Nara**) was made the first 'permanent' capital. Laid out in the grid-style pattern of Ch'ang an, the Chinese capital of the time, **Heijō-kyō** became a large prosperous city.

The increasing power of the Buddhist temples was seen as a threat to the power of the emperor. One of the later rulers, **Kammu**, decided to move the capital to **Heian-kyō** (present-day **Kyōto**). **Kyōto** remained the official capital of Japan until the 19th century.

*The first **Kasuga** Shrine was built in 768 by the **Fujiwara** clan. It is famous today for its lanterns, about two-thirds of which are stone and the rest bronze.*

The Heian Period (AD 794–1192)

*This stamp shows a scene from **Genji Monogatari** (The Tale of Prince Genji), a classic of Japanese literature and the world's first novel. The author was **Murasaki Shikibu** (c.978–c.1015). She wrote about the **Minamoto** court.*

The move to **Heian-kyō** was the beginning of the **Heian** (Peace) period during which the inhabitants, originally descendants of Korean, Chinese and other Asian peoples, began to see themselves as one people. The feeling of national identity was strengthened by a fall in the number of immigrants.

At the wealthy imperial court, the arts and literature were encouraged. The court lifestyle was extravagant, while the people who worked the land were very poor. There was widespread corruption and unrest. Imperial power began to shift to local leaders, in particular the **Fujiwara** clan.

In the mid-12th century, the **Taira** clan rose to power momentarily, but they were defeated in 1185 by the army of **Minamoto Yoritomo** who became the first **shōgun** ('army leader').

The Kamakura Period (AD 1192–1336)

Minamoto Yoritomo set up his base in **Kamakura**, far from **Kyōto** and the imperial court. As a powerful military leader, the **shōgun** controlled the country. The emperor had no power, but remained as a figurehead. The **shōgun** handed power to his son, until control was taken by another ambitious military leader.

A century later, the Mongols tried to invade Japan. In 1281, Kublai Khan brought a great fleet of ships with 100,000 soldiers from China. Near **Hakata** in northern **Kyūshū**, a typhoon blew up and sank many of the ships. The Japanese called the typhoon **kamikaze** or 'the divine wind.'

Despite the failure of the invasion, there was discontent among the **samurai** warriors and they withdrew their support for the **shōgun**. In 1333, Emperor **Godaigo** made a successful attempt to regain power.

Samurai ('People who serve') were something like knights in medieval Western Europe. They swore loyalty to one of the many warlords and fought for him.

*Zen Buddhism provided the **samurai** with **bushidō**, a spiritual code which influenced even their approach to the martial arts.*

Unity and isolation

The Muromachi Period (1336–1573)

After a short time the military leaders withdrew their support for Emperor **Godaigo**. He was forced to flee to the **Yoshino** mountains near **Nara**. Shōgun **Ashikaga Takauji** then set up a new emperor, **Kōmyō**, in **Kyōto**.

From 1336 to 1392, there were two emperors, one in **Kyōto** and another in **Yoshino**. Finally, a successor of **Godaigo** gave up his claim to the throne, leaving only the **Kyōto** emperor.

The military leaders remained in control until the last half of the 16th century. During this time, small areas of land came under the control of **daimyō**, or local warlords. Using the **samurai** loyal to him (see pages 16–17), each **daimyō** fought to gain

more territory and increase his power.

When the **shōgun** was no longer able to control the activities of the **daimyō**, a civil war lasting a hundred years broke out.

*During the **Muromachi** period, garden design developed. The features included hills, waterfalls, streams, islands, bridges and stones, all arranged to imitate nature in a subtle way and to appear 'natural.'*

The Momoyama Period (1573–1598)

*Christianity was brought to Japan through **Kyūshū** in 1549. When Saint Francis Xavier, a Spanish Catholic priest, introduced the new religion, it was welcomed at first and hundreds of Japanese became Christians. Later, Christianity was banned because it was thought that Spain or Portugal would use the new religion to help the Pope colonize Japan. Japanese Christians were persecuted and killed.*

In 1573, **Nobunaga Oda** defeated the **daimyō** living around his land near present-day **Nagoya**. Then, he marched to **Kyōto** to take power. Before his assassination in 1582, he had attempted to dominate—and reunite—Japan.

After his death, one of his generals, **Hideyoshi Toyotomi** took power. His tact in dealing with the **daimyō** made sure that the country remained stable.

*Each **daimyō** built castles to defend his territory. **Himeji Jō** (Himeji Castle) was built by **Hideyoshi Toyotomi** in 1581.*

The Edo Period (1603–1867)

After **Hideyoshi Toyotomi** died, there was a battle to see who would be the next **shōgun**. **Ieyasu Tokugawa** (1542–1616) fought his way to power, suppressing all opposition. His **bakufu** (shogunate) was based at **Edo**, on the site of modern **Tōkyō**. The local **samurai** were allocated land in return for loyalty to **Tokugawa**.

To keep the **daimyō** under control **Tokugawa** forced their families to live permanently in **Edo**. They were effectively hostages.

The **Tokugawa** clan considered any influence from abroad as a threat to its power and thousands of Christians were martyred. In 1639, trade and contact with foreign countries were banned, although a tiny settlement of Dutch traders remained on the island of **Dejima**, just off **Nagasaki**. For more than two centuries, it was the only link with the outside world.

Any Japanese returning from abroad was executed so that no outside influences might disturb the structured society that was to be controlled by the **Tokugawa** family for 250 years.

*Although Japan was officially closed to foreigners, an English sailor, Will Adams (1564–1620), became an adviser on Europe and shipbuilding to **Ieyasu Tokugawa**. (Adams came to Japan in 1598 with a Dutch trading expedition.) He was given an estate near **Edo** and lived the rest of his life in Japan.*

◀ *During the **Edo** period, social classes were rigidly defined. They included **samurai**, farmers and merchants. Laws regulated everyday life, even the hairstyles and the kind of food people could eat. Despite the strict controls, it was a time of peace and stability.*

*The famous artist **Hokusai Katsushika** (1760–1849) drew and painted many aspects of life in **Edo**, including this street scene.*

(A) Find a book with more pictures by **Hokusai**. What differences can you see between life in Japan and Europe or America in the 18th century?

Despite the inflexibility of society in the ▶ ***Edo** period, it saw the development of **kabuki** drama and many of the fine crafts that are now regarded as fundamental to the culture of Japan.*

*This carving (right) is in the **Tōshōgū** Shrine at **Nikkō**. The shrine was built as a memorial to **Ieyasu Tokugawa**.*

Modern times

The Meiji Period (1868–1912)

For over 250 years, Japan had been closed to the outside world. From limited trading contacts with other countries, the Japanese realized that they were falling behind technologically. The first effective move to break the isolation came from outside. In 1853, Commodore Perry from the United States established diplomatic relations with Japan.

Closer contact with other countries was not the only change. The **bakufu** (shogunate) was becoming weaker and gave up power to the opposition forces who supported the emperor. Emperor **Meiji** came to the throne in 1867. He was brought to **Edo** (later renamed **Tōkyō**) and was reinstated as the leader of the nation. Within three years, the **daimyō** (warlords) had submitted to the new government in **Tōkyō**

Commodore Matthew Perry arrived in **Uraga** Bay in 1853. As well as wanting to trade, the American government needed ports in Japan where its steamships could refuel with coal after the long Pacific crossing. The Japanese called the American fleet the 'black ships.'

There was rapid change during the **Meiji** period. Japan welcomed innovations from abroad, but lost some of its culture in the process. New industries, a railway network and an educational system were developed. A parliament, based on Western European and American government systems, was set up.

With modern weapons, the Japanese military became particularly strong. Shortages of raw materials and the search for new markets in which to sell its goods led Japan to war with China (1894–5) and Russia (1904–5).

(Above) Japanese sailors take part in the naval battle of **Tsushima** in 1905. The Russian fleet suffered a total defeat.

日本語

Numbers often appear as we write them, as well as in **kanji** (characters).

1	一	**ichi**
2	二	**ni**
3	三	**san**
4	四	**shi** or **yon**
5	五	**go**
6	六	**roku**
7	七	**shichi** or **nana**
	八	**hachi**
	九	**kyū** or **ku**
	十	**jū**

Numbers from 11 to 99 are formed by making combinations of tens and other numbers.

For example:

11	十一	**jū-ichi**
12	十二	**jū-ni**
20	二十	**ni-jū**
21	二十一	**ni-jū-ichi**
30	三十	**san-jū**
40	四十	**yon-jū**
50	五十	**go-jū**
65	六十五	**roku-jū-go**
79	七十九	**nana-jū-kyū**
87	八十七	**hachi-jū-nana**
99	九十九	**kyū-jū-kyū**

1 Write the following numbers in Japanese, first in **rōmaji**, then in **kanji**:
a 26
b 47
c 59
d 33
e 85

Overseas empire and World War II

The reign of Emperor **Taishō** (1912–1926) and the early part of his successor, **Hirohito's**, was relatively calm as Japan's new democratic system began to develop. However, when political corruption became widespread and an economic depression began, the military increased its control again.

*In the seven years following the war, the Allied forces under American General MacArthur imposed a new social structure. **Shintō**, the religion closely associated with militarism, began to fade. A democratic government was installed again and women were given the vote.*

Conquests of Asian countries followed, most notably China. (Korea had already been taken over by Japan in 1910.) Manchuria in north-eastern China was occupied in 1931 and six years later a full-scale invasion of China was launched.

Relations with the West also took a turn for the worse. The Japanese surprise attack on the American fleet in Pearl Harbor on December 8, 1941, took Japan into World War II. After nearly four years of hard fighting in south-east Asia, Japan suffered its first national military defeat.

Many cities were bombed and atomic bombs were dropped on **Hiroshima** and **Nagasaki**. The final surrender came on August 15, 1945, after the Emperor spoke to the nation.

*Hirohito was emperor for 63 years from 1926 to 1989. Like Emperor **Taishō** before him, **Hirohitō** witnessed great changes. Before World War II he was considered a 'living God;' afterwards he was merely a symbol of the Japanese state.*

The Japanese people suffered much hardship after the war, as they rebuilt their country. But within 25 years, the combined efforts of the government and industry had made Japan one of the world's greatest industrial economies.

——— 日本語 ———

The months of the year also use numbers. (See page 20.)

ichigatsu	一月	January
nigatsu	二月	February
sangatsu	三月	March
shigatsu	四月	April
gogatsu	五月	May
rokugatsu	六月	June
shichigatsu	七月	July
hachigatsu	八月	August
kugatsu	九月	September
jūgatsu	十月	October
jūichigatsu	十一月	November
jūnigatsu	十二月	December

☐ If someone asks you what month it is:

Nangatsu desu ka?

. . . look at the list of months and put the correct month into this sentence.

. . .*desu.*

What's the date?

- When Japanese people write a date, they start with the year. For example, September 28, 1992, would be written as:

1992年 9 月28日

The **kanji** 月 for 'month' also means **tsuki** (moon); 日 means **nichi** (day) and **hi** (sun).

- Sometimes, the year is given in terms of the emperor's reign. The present reign, known as **Heisei** (平成), began in 1989 when **Akihito** became emperor. The year 1992 is year 4 of **Heisei**, so September 28, 1992, could also be written:

平成 4 年 9 月28日

[2] What is this date?   91 年09 月02 日

(A) Write today's date the Japanese way:
  a giving the year in the usual form.
  b using **Heisei**.
(B) Write the day and the month of your **tanjōbi** (birthday) the Japanese way.

At school and university

Gakkō

Gakkō (school) starts with **shōgakkō** (elementary school) at six. From the age of 13 to 15, students attend **chūgakkō** (junior high school). Although not compulsory, most students stay on after 15 for a three-year course at **kōtōgakkō** (senior high school). There are both single-sex and coeducational schools, and a large number of private schools.

The school year is divided into three terms April–July, September–December and January–March. Classes with as many as 50 students are usual at **chūgakkō** and **kōtōgakkō**, but discipline is maintained because students want to do well in their exams.

The idea of passing exams dominates everything. Students who fall behind or want to increase their chances of passing exams go to a **juku** (tutor) for more intensive study after school.

Eigo to kokugo . . .

School lessons last 50 minutes. Here are some of the subjects the students study in class:

Eigo	英語	English
Kokugo	国語	Japanese (literally 'national language')
Sūgaku	数学	Mathematics
Rika	理科	Science
Rekishi	歴史	History
Ongaku	音楽	Music
Chiri	地理	Geography
Bijutsu	美術	Art

Left: At ***chūgakkō****, and* ***kōtōgakkō****, everyone learns* ***Eigo*** *(English). An increasing number of students go abroad to study in the USA, the UK or Australia.*

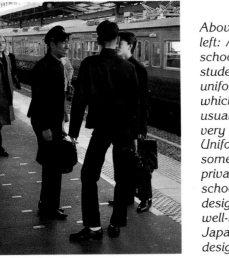

Above and left: All school students wear uniforms, which they usually keep very neat. Uniforms for some girls' private schools are designed by well-known Japanese designers.

--- 日本語 ---

(Eigo) o benkyō shimasu ka?
〔英語〕をべんきょうしますか。
Do you study (English)?

Hai. Benkyō shimasu.
はい。べんきょうします。
Yes, I do study it.

Iie. Benkyō shimasen.
いいえ。べんきょうしません。
No, I don't study it.

☐ With a partner.
Ask your partner about the subjects he or she studies. If you want to ask about learning Japanese, use the word **Nihongo**.

Kurabu

*High-school students like to stay after school to attend one or more after-school **kurabu** (clubs). The girls above are at a brass-band practice. A wide variety of **kurabu** includes sports, music and traditional Japanese pastimes such as calligraphy and flower arranging.*

Students also help to keep their classrooms clean and tidy after school hours.

Watashi no yume

What would your dream job be? Read what these students want to be. What would you like to be?

Anata no yume wa nan desu ka?

Watashi wa shashinka ni naritai desu.

Watashi wa sensei ni naritai desu.

joyū/haiyū	actress/actor
sensei	teacher
hisho	secretary
shashinka	photographer
isha	doctor
kaisha-in	office worker

Daigaku to semmon gakkō

If **kōtōgakkō** students can get through 'examination hell' with good marks, they have a chance to go to the best **daigaku** (universities) in **Tōkyō** or **Kyōto**. The big companies, especially **sōgō shōsha** (see page 26), recruit directly from the top universities.

Once at university, **semmon gakkō** (vocational college) or other higher education institutions, the pressure is off. As long as the student's attendance is satisfactory and the minimum amount of course work is covered, it is not difficult to graduate. Usually, students about to graduate are helped in their search for jobs.

1 What are the names of these two colleges where Japanese students can study English? One is in the USA and the other is in Australia. The **kanji** (character) for **daigaku** is 大学. (See the **katakana** chart on page 79.)

a カリフォルニア大学バークレイ

b シドニー大学

アイスクリームを
いかがですか。

2 Look at the photograph of the student doing part-time work. He is asking if you would like something. What is it? (See pages 78–79.)

As well as studying, many students do part-time jobs for pocket money. Sometimes, they are criticized for not taking their college work seriously enough. In a survey, more than 50 percent of students admitted they studied for two hours or less each day (in the library or at home), while 35 percent said they didn't study at all!

At work

O shigoto

Look at these photos of people doing their **shigoto** (work). If you want to ask someone what their job is, say:

O shigoto wa nan desu ka?

Ten-in desu.

Suchuwādesu desu.

スチュワーデスです。

Kangofu desu.

かんごふです。

てんいんです。

Shūrikō desu.

しゅうりこうです。

--- 日本語 ---

This is how you tell the time in Japanese. See page 20 for numbers.

Ichi-ji	一時	One o'clock
San-ji han	三時半	Half past three
Yo-ji ni-juppun	四時二十分	4.20
Go-ji yon-jū-gofun	五時四十五分	5.45
Roku-ji go-jū-sanpun	六時五十三分	6.53

Nan-ji ni shigoto o hajimemasu ka?
なん時にしごとを
はじめますか。
What time do you start work?

Ku-ji ni hajimemasu.
九時にはじめます。
I start at nine o'clock.

Nan-ji ni shigoto o owarimasu ka?
なん時にしごとをおわりますか。
What time do you finish work?

Shichi-ji jū-gofun ni owarimasu.
七時十五分におわります。
I finish work at 7:15.

☐ Say these times in Japanese:

a **7.10**　b **2.36**

c **8.05**　d **11.12**

e **10.00**

f 　g

Satō-san no ichinichi

Here are photos which give an idea of the Japanese working day. This is **Satō-san's** day.

7.50 a.m.
Shichi-ji go-juppun
七時五十分

"*I leave home at 7:25 a.m. and catch a train to work. Many commuters travel up to three hours a day to and from their place of work.*"

8.50 a.m.
Hachi-ji go-juppun
八時五十分

"*I must punch in before 9 a.m. All office workers have to punch in.*"

12.15 p.m.
Jū-ni-ji jū-gofun
十二時十五分

"*I usually eat a **bentō** (boxed lunch) at my desk.*"

6.35 p.m.
Roku-ji san-jū-gofun
六時三十五分

"*I usually get away at 6:30 p.m., but it can be later if my boss is still here. Then I'll wait until he goes.*"

8.00 p.m.
Hachi-ji
八時

"*About once a week, I have a drink after work with my coworkers.*"

12.10 a.m.
Jū-ni-ji juppun
十二時十分

"*When I go home late on the last train, it is nearly as crowded as the one I take in the morning.*"

(A) Draw up a plan to explain to someone what you do every day. Write the time of each activity in Japanese.

If you can write about any of the activities in Japanese, then do so. If not, write in English.

25

Made in Japan

Sōgō shōsha

Since World War II, Japan has become a leading industrial nation and Japanese companies have offices all over the world. About half of the working population in Japan is employed by large companies.

These companies are often part of **sōgō shōsha** which are powerful industrial and financial groups. The activities of **sōgō shōsha** may range from areas as diverse as banking, insurance and real estate to mining, ship-building and electronics.

Japan has few natural raw materials. In order to overcome the disadvantage of having to import so many raw materials, the country aims to make reliable, high-quality products to sell abroad. Japan is the world's leading producer of passenger cars, televisions and synthetic fibers.

One of the large industrial groups is **Mitsubishi**. *The company logo has three diamonds in it, because the name means 'three diamonds.' (See the section on numbers on page 55.)*

Ⓐ Do you know the origins of other Japanese company names? (For example, **Fuji** and **Sakura**.)

◀ *Japanese companies pioneered the large-scale use of robots in factories. More than two thirds of all the world's industrial robots are now installed in Japan.*

Left is a modern car plant where robots assemble some parts of motor vehicles.

More than four million people ▶ *work in agriculture. Except in* **Hokkaidō**, *farms are usually small, and many farmers make a living by combining farming with other part-time jobs.*

Rice is a major crop that has been a staple food for Japanese people for centuries. On smaller farms, rice shoots are still planted by hand.

Aidia no mise

Japan is a real **aidia no mise** ('idea shop'). New products are being developed all the time. Some ideas appeal particularly to Japanese people; there may be capsule hotel units with just enough space and the minimum facilities necessary for a one-night stay, a Buddhist altar which automatically plays recordings of prayers when someone kneels in front of it, or ready-cooked hamburgers sold from vending machines.

Some ideas may have seemed a little unusual at first, but later became popular in other countries. One of these was the **karaoke** machine which provides the musical backing for people to sing along to their favorite songs.

Capsule hotel rooms are equipped with a television, a radio and an alarm clock.

*A portable **karaoke** machine* ▶

Kaisha-in

One of the reasons for Japan's economic success is thought to be the way that people work together. Generally, Japanese **kaisha-in** (company employees) display a strong sense of loyalty. Cooperation to maintain **wa**, the harmony of the group, and collective effort are considered more important than personal ambition.

The majority of male **kaisha-in** stay with the same company until they retire at the age of 55 or 60. Women are not expected to have any long-term ambitions and usually give up working when their first child is due.

It is not unusual for **kaisha-in** to be moved to a different department. The company will train them for the new job.

Occasional weekend office trips (with the boss, too) help reinforce the sense of belonging to a group.

*The larger **kaisha** (companies) recruit most of their higher level white-collar workers among those about to graduate from university. The **kaisha-in** are selected on the basis of who is most likely to fit in rather than those with special skills or outstanding ability.*

Even after working in a company for many years, some **kaisha-in** may not be promoted to executive level. As it is rare for someone to be dismissed, these **kaisha-in** are given some relatively unimportant work to do. They are sometimes called **madogiwa zoku** because they are given desks by **mado** (the window) to pass their time pleasantly looking out the window or reading the newspaper.

Time off

Eiga

Going to see **eiga** (films) is a popular pastime. Younger people prefer the latest foreign (mostly American) movies, with subtitles in Japanese. Renting videos is also increasingly popular.

*An **eigakan** (cinema) in **Tōkyō**.*
とうきょうのえいがかん。 ▶

1. Can you find the name of the American film star and the film in the poster on the right? (Use the **katakana** chart on page 79 to help you.)

Hima

Here are some ways for people to spend **hima** (free time).

Pachinko is very popular. It is a kind of pinball game that takes its name from the sound that the metal balls make as they go round the machine.

Concentrating on a game of **pachinko** helps people to forget about a hard day at work. **Pachinko** prize tokens can be exchanged for cash at nearby shops.

In a commuter train you are just as likely to see students or commuters reading **manga** (comic books) as **shinbun** (newspapers). People also spend hours browsing through the latest **manga**, **zasshi** (magazines) or **hon** (books) in bookshops. Some even read the magazines from cover to cover! Browsing is so common there is a special word for it — **tachiyomi**.

Another way to unwind at the end of the day is **karaoke**, singing along to the music of your favorite song. There even are tour buses fitted with **karaoke** systems (with words and pictures displayed on a TV screen) to while away the time spent in traffic jams.

A lot of Japanese homes have two or three
elevisions. On **terebi** (television) there's a choice
of up to seven regular channels in addition to
atellite and cable stations. **NHK**, the state
elevision network, runs two channels without
advertising. Other commercial stations put out a
mixture of game shows, drama, news, sports and
music programs.

Samurai dramas, set in old Japan, have many
ans, young and old. Popular TV hosts and
omedians have daily shows and often appear as
uests on other programs, as well as in TV ads.

Although films shown on television are
mostly dubbed into Japanese, some can be
njoyed in the original on televisions with a
bilingual facility. Some news broadcasts and
American **hōmu dorama** (soap operas) can also
be heard in English.

	時	
05回'90ツール・ド・フラン ス「フランスが世界に 誇る自転車レース」	00 わんぱく相撲全国大会 鈴木桂一郎 内山範子 ～両国国技館（録画）	**4**
00 N◇05回サマー・アイ ドル「光ゲンジ・オン ・ステージ」◇55回市	00 セサミストリート国 「ヒロシのアトリエ」 ジェーン・カーチンほか	**5**
00 経済マガジン「イラク 撤退表明・どう動く中 東情勢・第3次石油危 機は来るか」◇45N天	00 リビングナウ「トイレ は健康管理室」 30 世界の職人芸 40 聴力障害者の時間	**6**
00 7時のニュース◇天 20 クイズ百点満点「好景 気が44カ月も続く日本 調べる方法と人は？身 近な実感から〝景気〟 を」田畑彦右衛門ほか	00 フランス語会話国 「プチスケッチ集」 小林茂ほか◇27花の風景 スペイン語会話国 30 「授業が終わったとこ ろです」東谷頴人	**7**

NHKテレビ①   **NHK教育テレビ③**

Look at this listing for NHK channels 1 and 3 from the
Asahi Shinbun newspaper.

2 Sometimes a Roman letter is used to indicate a
news program. What do you think it is?

3 The **kanji** for **tenki** (weather) is 天気. How many
weather bulletins can you find? At what times are
they shown?

4 Think of how a Japanese person might say the
words underlined below. Using your knowledge of
katakana and the chart on pages 78–79, write the
words in **katakana**.

a *Living now*
b A quiz show
c The *Tour de France* cycle race
d *Sesame Street*
e The news
f A pop **aidoru** in concert (*On stage*)

5 Look at the program listing to find out at what
time (and on which channel) you can view the
programs above.

日本語

or the days of the week, the **kanji** (characters)
nd literal meanings are given beside the **romaji**.

Nichiyōbi	（日曜日 SUN-day）	Sunday
Getsuyōbi	（月曜日 MOON-day）	Monday
Kayōbi	（火曜日 FIRE-day）	Tuesday
Suiyōbi	（水曜日 WATER-day）	Wednesday
Mokuyōbi	（木曜日 WOOD-day）	Thursday
Kinyōbi	（金曜日 GOLD-day）	Friday
Doyōbi	（土曜日 EARTH-day）	Saturday

Ryokō

Most people are only able to
take a long **ryokō** (trip) during
Gōruden uiiku (Golden Week),
which is from April 29 to May
5, or in the middle of August
when a lot of companies are
closed. Trains and flights at
these times are fully booked well
in advance.

In Japan, **Okinawa**, **Hokkaidō**
and **Nagano** Prefecture attract
many visitors, but it is often less
expensive to go abroad to Hong
Kong or Guam in the Pacific.

*Japanese tourists traveling
outside Japan prefer pack-
age tours so they can
make the most of their 10-
or 12-day trips. There are
special retirement tours to
Europe or the USA. Hawaii
is a favorite place for
honeymoons.*

*On **shūmatsu** (week-
ends), people like to get
out of crowded cities to
visit hot spring resorts and
beaches. Some families
have second homes in the
mountains.*

Literature, music and art

Hon

◀ Children read **hon** (books) such as those by **Ryuno-suke Akutagawa** (1892–1927). Some of his stories are borrowed from Japanese legends.

Notice how this book opens. Because Japanese writing is usually written from top to bottom and right to left, the books opens the same way.

Japanese writers with an international reputation include the winner of the 1968 Nobel Prize for Literature, **Yasunari Kawabata** (1899–1972) and **Yukio Mishima** (1925–1970).

Novels by **Kawabata** feature a sense of alienation and loss. They include **Senbazuru** (Thousand Cranes) and **Utsukushisa to kanashimi** (Beauty and Sadness). **Yukio Mishima** wrote stories and novels about the difficulty of reconciling things of the mind and of the body. His book **Gogo no eikō** (1963) was filmed in 1974 as The Sailor who fell from Grace with the Sea.

> Kono michi ya
> Yuku hito nashi ni
> Aki no kure

> This road
> No one walks along it
> Dusk in autumn

This is a **haiku**, a short poem of exactly 17 syllables (five syllables on the first line, seven on the second and five on the third.) with its English translation. Many **haiku** are written about nature. The simple style helps suggest a mood and a deeper meaning.

(A) Write your own **haiku** in English. Remember to include a word linked to one of the seasons.

Ongaku

You may hear traditional **ongaku** (music) in a variety of places. Visitors to performances of **kabuki** and traditional music concerts have a chance to hear instruments such as the 13-stringed **koto**, the **shamisen** (a three-stringed lute) or the **shakuhachi**, a bamboo flute. The **koto** is played by plucking the strings with a pick. The **shamisen** is held like a guitar, but only the three middle fingers are used to hold down the strings. Recordings of traditional music are played in some restaurants and even in supermarkets.

Shakuhachi ▶
しゃくはち

◀ *Koto* こと

Sumi-e

Although many Japanese artists paint in oils and watercolors, the traditional style of painting is **sumi-e**. These **e** (paintings) are made using **sumi** (ink) on paper.

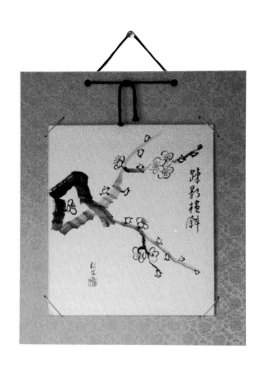

In the centuries before pens were used in Japan, people wrote with **fude** (brushes). The same word **kaku** is used to mean 'to draw' and 'to write.'

Shodō

Shodō (Calligraphy) is the art of writing an elegant, but individual version of a **kanji** (character). **Ai**, the **kanji** for 'love' (above left) is a favourite subject for **shodō**. An ordinary printed version is on the right.

The order in which the strokes of a **kanji** are written is very important. The **kanji** above form the name **Tōkyō** (東京). The numbers indicate the stroke order.

B Look at the **hiragana** and **katakana** charts on pages 78–79. Find a firm brush and some black poster paint. Write out some of the **hiragana** and **katakana** with a brush. Then write them with a pen. What differences do you notice between writing with a brush and with a pen?

C With a brush, practice writing these **kanji** until you have one you would like to hang on the wall.

Holidays and festivals

Saijitsu

During the year there are 14 **saijitsu** or official national holidays when most offices and factories are closed. Shops stay open, except over the New Year.

Seijin no hi せいじんのひ

Seijin no hi (Coming of Age Day): January 15 is a celebration for everyone who has reached the age of 20 in the past year. Many girls dress up in traditional **kimono**.

Midori no hi (Greenery Day)/ **Kempō Kinembi** (Constitution Day)/**Kodomo no hi** (Children's Day): These holidays fall so close together (on April 29, May 3 and 5) that most people can look forward to a week's holiday —**Gōruden uiiku** (Golden Week). (See page 29).

On **Kodomo no hi**, originally called **Tango no sekku** (Boys' Day), huge **koi** (carp) streamers made of cloth are displayed.

Other **saijitsu** include **Keirō no hi** (Respect for the Aged Day) on September 15 and **Tennō tanjōbi** (Emperor's Birthday) on December 23.

Matsuri

Some of the most important **matsuri** (festivals) which are celebrated throughout Japan are:

Setsubun (February 3 or 4): People throw handfuls of dried beans around their homes to drive out evil spirits and bring good fortune. This is a Buddhist ritual which is also carried out at shrines and temples.

Hina Matsuri (March 3): A festival for girls, when a set of dolls dressed in ancient costumes are displayed on shelves covered in red cloth. Peach-blossom twigs are used as decoration.

Tanabata (July 7): This Star Festival commemorates the love of a princess and a farm hand who were only allowed to meet once a year. Children write their wishes on strips of paper and tie them to bamboo branches.

O bon (July 13–16 or August 13–16): A Buddhist festival when the spirits of ancestors are supposed to return. People return to their home towns to visit relatives. Everyone in the neighborhood gets together for the **bon odori** (community dancing).

Tanabata たなばた

Shichi-go-san (November 15): Seven-year-old girls, five-year-old boys and three-year-old girls are dressed up. The girls, and sometimes their mothers, wear **kimono**. The children go with their parents to shrines to pray for good luck.

◀ *Shichi-go-san* しちごさん

1 Look at the name of the November **matsuri**. What does the name mean in English? (See page 20 for numbers.)

O shōgatsu

O shōgatsu (New Year) is the most important Japanese celebration. Only **Ganjitsu** (January 1) is an official national holiday, but nearly everyone is off work from January 1 to the following week. People eat **o sechi ryōri**, traditional food that is prepared before the holiday and served cold, so the cook can have a rest, too!

During the first three days of the New Year, people visit shrines and get together with relatives. Children receive **o toshidama** (gifts of money) from relatives.

On **Ō misoka** (New Year's Eve), some people go to Buddhist temples where, around midnight, the bell is rung 108 times to represent the sins of the old year.

*Pine, bamboo and plum branch decorations called **kadomatsu** can be seen everywhere, especially outside houses.*

(A) Make a calendar with two columns. One column is headed **Nihon** and the other one with the Japanese name for the country where you live.

Write down the main public holidays and festivals in Japan, then write down the ones that happen in your country. Are some festivals taking place in both countries at the same time?

O mikoshi

As well as the major **matsuri**, there are local festivals. The young men of the area carry an **o mikoshi** (portable shrine) through the streets, chanting as they go.

Some of the best-known regional **matsuri** are:

Tsurugaoka Hachimangū Matsuri (April 7–14): This spring **matsuri** takes place at the largest shrine in **Kamakura** in the **sakura** (cherry blossom) viewing season.

Gion Matsuri: Held during July at the **Yasaka** Shrine in **Kyōto**, this is said to date back over a thousand years. On July 17, there is a procession of floats.

Kantō Matsuri (August 5–7) and **Nebuta Matsuri** (August 3–7) are two of the biggest summer festivals in the **Tōhoku** region. They feature large, illuminated papier mâché dolls and animals.

O mikoshi ▶
おみこし

Okurimono

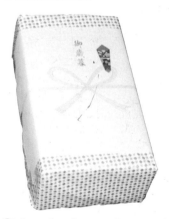

*Giving **okurimono** (presents) is a way of life in Japan. During O **chūgen** (just before **O bon**) and **O seibo** (in December) the custom is to give **okurimono** to people like bosses, clients and landlords. For people who have to send a lot of **okurimono**, **depāto** (department stores) offer a delivery service.*

(B) At what time of year do you give gifts to people? Are these the same as in Japan or different?

Religion

Shintō to Bukkyō

Although the majority of Japanese people say that they have no deep religious beliefs, traditions from **Shintō** (Shinto) and **Bukkyō** (Buddhism) exist side by side in everyday life. Usually, there are **Shintō** rituals for birth, coming-of-age and marriage, but funerals are Buddhist. About one percent of Japanese people are Christians.

Until the 12th century, **Bukkyō** was only followed by the ruling classes, but it did influence Japanese art and culture strongly. **Shintō** was the state religion from the **Meiji** Restoration in the 19th century until 1946 when a new constitution guaranteed freedom of worship.

Shintō priests. **Shintō** means 'the way of the gods' and has a history going back thousands of years. Originally, people worshipped **kami**, gods which were believed to live in trees, mountains, waterfalls and other natural objects. Later, the emperor, some warriors and important people were also worshiped as gods.

People visit the graves of their relatives at **O bon** (see pages 32–33), on Spring Equinox Day in March and on the anniversary of the person's death. They bring flowers and often a small amount of the deceased's favourite food.

(A) Are any customs on these pages like ones in your country?

Weddings usually take place at hotels. There is a **Shintō** ceremony which is often held at a shrine in the hotel. The bride first wears a silk kimono, then changes into a long white dress and veil in time to cut the cake. Rather than giving wedding presents, guests offer a specially decorated envelope containing money to help with the enormous cost of the wedding.

Followers of Zen, a Buddhist sect. **Bukkyō** (Buddhism) originated in India about 2,600 years ago. The religion is named after its founder, Gautauma Siddhartha, who was known as Buddha or 'the Enlightened One.' The basic ideas of **Bukkyō** are tolerance, equality and enlightenment. Buddhism came to Japan in AD 538 by way of China and Korea.

Jinja to otera

Jinja (**Shintō** shrines) and **otera** (Buddhist temples) may look alike, but only **jinja** have special **torii** (gateways) to keep away evil spirits. A symbol in the shape of a **torii** is used to show the position of a **Shintō** shrine on a map.

Prayers come in many forms; students preparing for important examinations can ask for prayers to be faxed to them.

Torii とりい

The purpose of the **tsurigane** *(hanging bell) at an* **otera** *was originally to ring out the hours because people did not have clocks.*

When people go the **otera** *and* **jinja** *they throw coins into a* **saisenbako** *(offertory box) and make a wish. People also pay for prayers to be written and put up. Some buy* **o mikuji**, *strips of white paper with predictions. Tying* **o mikuji** *to trees helps bring good fortune or drive away bad luck.*

At the temple, people purify themselves with the smoke from incense.

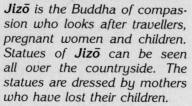

Jizō is the Buddha of compassion who looks after travellers, pregnant women and children. Statues of Jizō can be seen all over the countryside. The statues are dressed by mothers who have lost their children.

Three- or five-story pagoda are found in the grounds of Buddhist temples. They are said to contain a small part of the ashes of Gautama Siddhartha. The five roofs represent earth, fire, water, wind and air.

The Japanese way

New and old

Modern Japan

Everywhere you look in Japan's big cities, you can see concrete buildings, expressways, hamburger shops and other signs of a lifestyle as modern as any in the world. This can make visitors think that the Japanese way of doing things is no longer followed. Of course, many old customs are disappearing as a new society emerges. The older generation, struggling to keep up with the changes, is sometimes unhappy about their grandchildren's indifference to the old culture.

Generally though, the Japanese are known for their ability to borrow ideas from other countries and adapt them to suit their lifestyle. People can choose from the old and the new. Families living in modern houses still take off their shoes before entering and may use chopsticks when eating western food.

Older people in Japan are concerned that the younger generation has less respect for the values of hard work and co-operation which helped Japanese society through difficult times in its history.

*This boy is wearing a plastic version of the topknot hairstyle that the **samurai** warriors used to wear.*

Insiders and outsiders

The idea of **wa**, or group harmony, runs through Japanese society. It applies to any group of Japanese people: families, those who work together, even tourists travelling together in a foreign country. The group is more important than the individual.

There can, however, be a negative side, as anyone considered an 'outsider' may be ignored or even discriminated against. **Burakumin** have been an isolated group in Japan for centuries because originally they worked as in the leather trade and did other jobs considered 'unclean'. Even today, they often have no choice but to live in separate districts.

It is almost impossible for **gaijin** (foreigners) to be fully accepted into Japanese society. The largest racial minority group is the Koreans and there is also a sizable Chinese community. During World War II, 600,000 Koreans were brought to Japan, but even third-generation Koreans are not allowed to be Japanese citizens.

*Japanese people have a saying: **Deru kugi wa utareru**. It means literally 'the nail that sticks up is hammered down' and suggests the idea of not pushing yourself forward too much as an individual.*

Sumimasen!

Japanese politeness is legendary, although when commuters on a crowded train push each other it may seem hard to believe. The Japanese are always courteous to people to whom they have been introduced.

Politeness, even if only superficial, can be seen in everyday situations. When a department store opens in the morning the sales clerks line up near the door and bow to the customers.

There are special words to show respect for other people or things. You may notice in this book that some words have **o** before them, such as **o hashi** for chopsticks or **o cha** for green tea (see pages 52–53 and 54–55). There are also polite words for talking about someone else's family (see pages 60–61).

- Apologising for something:

Gomen nasai.
ごめんなさい。
I'm so sorry (for the trouble I have caused).

- When one person leaves another, when finishing work or getting off a train, he or she will say **Shitsurei shimasu**. This means literally 'I will be rude' and is used instead of **sayonara**.

Shitsurei shimasu.

*The most formal way of thanking someone is **Dōmo arigatō gozaimasu** (or **gozaimashita**).*

1 What other way of saying 'thank you' do you know in Japanese?

Takamiya sensei, sumimasen ga . . .

*When students speak to their teachers, they use the word **sensei** after the person's name or just **sensei**. **Sensei** is for teachers, doctors and others whom you respect.*

*If you need help, are taking up someone else's time, have trouble in communicating or want to express thanks, **sumimasen** is a useful word.*

Sign language—Japanese style

Here are some gestures that the Japanese make with their hands to emphasize what they are saying:

"Who, me?"

"Excuse me."

"Come here, quick!"

People

Yūmei na hito

Here are some Japanese **hito** (people) who are **yūmei na** (well-known).
Some are as famous in other countries as they are in Japan.

Seiji Ozawa おざわせいじ

Seiji Ozawa became assistant conductor of the New York Philharmonic Orchestra in 1960 after winning an international conducting contest.

As a young child, Seiji Ozawa learned many songs from his mother, but it was his elder brother who gave him his first lessons on the accordion and the piano.

After seeing a famous conductor at a concert at the age of 16, Seiji wanted to become a conductor himself. He graduated from music college in **Tōkyō** and spent some time with one of Japan's best orchestras, the NHK Symphony Orchestra. Then he went on to become the music director of the Boston Symphony Orchestra.

He also works with the **Saitō Kinen** Orchestra which performs for only three weeks every year. It is made up of Japanese musicians who play in orchestras round the world.

Akio Morita もりたあきお

To many people outside Japan the name of Akio Morita may be less well-known than the name of the company he helped found, Sony. His name is certainly familiar to most Japanese people.

Akio Morita attended **Ōsaka** University and later set up **Tōkyō** Telegraph Industries with a friend. The name was later changed to Sony which is based on the Latin word for 'sound'—*sonus*.

After experimenting with rice cookers and other household appliances, in 1957 the company launched the first successful transistor radio. It then went on develop a range of state-of-the-art electrical appliances, including televisions, hi-fi equipment and the personal stereo.

Akio Morita is a kind of 'industrial ambassador' who works toward improving trading relations between Japan and other countries, especially the United States.

Mitsuko Uchida うちだみつこ

Mitsuko Uchida is one of a growing number of talented Japanese classical musicians. She studied at the **Tōhō Gakuen** music school for children.

Because her father worked in the Japanese diplomatic service, the whole family moved to Europe when Mitsuko was 11. She continued her piano studies there, and later graduated from the Vienna Music Academy.

She has won many musical awards for her playing. With a base in London, she has toured the world with various orchestras, including Japan's NHK Symphony Orchestra. She is well-known for her recordings of Mozart and Beethoven.

Ever since designers Hanae Mori and Issey Miyake appeared on the international scene in the 1970s, Japanese fashion design has attracted attention.

After taking a design course and working for a fashion company in Tōkyō, Kenzō Takada went to work in the Paris fashion world. He set up his own business in 1970.

In 1984, Kenzō was nominated top designer by a panel of international journalists at the Paris Collections. People say that his clothes are popular because in his designs are a combination of European style and a delicate Japanese touch.

◀ *Kenzō Takada* たかだけんぞう

To television viewers in Japan the comedian Tamori is a very familiar face. Every Friday night, he hosts a popular variety show called *Tamori Kurabu* (*Tamori Club*). It features lighthearted interviews, music and other guest comedians. Tamori always appears on television wearing dark glasses.

His real name is Kazuyoshi Morita. He wanted to be a professional musician, but after his student days, he became an ordinary **sarariiman** (company employee) for a while. Then he broke into show business with a regular lunchtime show on television.

As well as appearing on television, Tamori makes records and writes books.

Tamori タモリ ▶

Japanese film directors Akira Kurosawa and Nagisa Ōshima are well-known abroad for films such as **Ran** *and* Merry Christmas Mr Lawrence. *But most films produced for Japan include pop* **aidoru** *(literally 'idols') for younger moviegoers and dramas for older people.*

Ⓐ Do you know the names of any other Japanese **yūmei na hito**? You may be able to find out about them from a newspaper. You could look in the:
 – international news
 – business news
 – sports pages
 – entertainment section

Namae wa?

When Japanese people give someone's full **namae** (name), they usually give the surname first. We say Kenzō Takada, but in Japan he would be called **Takada Kenzō**.

Japanese people have only one given name. Many girls' names end in **-ko** which means 'child.' Among the most common names for boys are **Hiroshi** which means 'wise, intelligent' and **Yoshio** which means 'good person.' A few names, such as **Hiromi**, are for girls and boys.

For signing names on official documents **hanko** (seals) are used. These show the **kanji** (characters) for the person's surname.

This is an enlarged print from a **hanko** *for the surname Ōsawa.*

1 Look at all the Japanese names on these pages. Write them out the Japanese way in **rōmaji** or in **hiragana** if you can.

Ⓑ Do you know any other Japanese names? Make two columns headed **Onna no ko no namae** (Girls' names) and **Otoko no ko no namae** (Boys' names). Write down the names that you know in the correct column.

39

Getting around town

Basu to densha

Within city boundaries, a flat-fare system is operated on **basu** (buses). To pay on the bus you put the correct fare into a tray near the driver or use the machine and get change. **Kai-sūken** (coupon tickets) are less expensive and can be bought at bus stations and some local shops.

The easiest and quickest way to get around the major cities, like **Tōkyō** and **Ōsaka**, is by **densha** (train) or **chika-tetsu** (subway).

Every stop on trains and buses is announced, but it may be difficult to catch the name of the place you want in the middle of all the extra information!

Boarding at the **basu tei** (bus stop).

The small white sign to the right of the door says **iriguchi** (entrance). 'Exit' is 出口 (**deguchi**).

To buy a **kippu** (ticket) for the train, find the station you want on the map above the ticket machine. Then put in coins for the right amount or more. The machines always give the correct change, even if you put in as much as a 10,000-yen note.

Densha (trains) are clean and punctual. Try to avoid the morning rush hour. This is the time when railway employees at some of the busiest stations 'help' passengers onto trains!

◀ This sign has the **kanji** (character) for **eki** (station).
ここはえきです。

Station names and signs in **rōmaji** and ▶ English are becoming more widespread, even outside **Tōkyō**. The name of this station **Ōtsuka** is written in **hiragana**, **kanji** and **rōmaji** to make sure you know where you are!

Jitensha to takushii

◀ *These **jitensha** (bicycles) are parked near a station. **Jitensha** are a convenient way of getting around town. To avoid traffic, people sometimes ride on sidewalks. Cyclists can ignore the usual traffic regulations, such as traffic lights or one-way streets.*

*You can hail **takushii** (taxis)* ▶ *in the street. A red light on the passenger side shows the **takushii** is available. The driver opens and closes the passenger door automatically, so stand clear if you are getting in. **Takushii** are expensive, but tips are not expected.*

If you want to go to Ginza, say:

Ginza made itte kudasai.

When you want the **takushii** to stop, say:

Koko de tomete kudasai.

日本語

Sumimasen. (Eki) wa doko desu ka?
すみません。〔えき〕はどこですか。
Excuse me. Where is the (station)?

Massugu itte kudasai.
まっすぐいってください。
Please go straight on.

Hidari e magatte kudasai.
ひだりへまがってください。
Please turn left.

Migi e magatte kudasai.
みぎへまがってください。
Please turn right.

Asoko no hidarigawa desu.
あそこのひだりがわです。
It's over there on the left.

Asoko no migigawa desu.
あそこのみぎがわです。
It's over there on the right.

(Shinjuku) made ikura desu ka?
〔しんじゅく〕までいくらですか。
How much is it to (**Shinjuku**)?

Kono basu wa (Ginza eki) e ikimasu ka?
このバスは〔ぎんざえき〕へいきますか。
Does this bus go to (**Ginza** Station)?

☐ You are at **Tōkyō eki**.
a Ask how much it is to these places:
 – **Ueno**
 – **Shibuya**
 – **Chiba**
 – **Yokohama**
b Ask if the train goes to each of the **eki** above.

Doko desu ka?

If you don't know where to go, or are lost, people are happy to help. But taxi drivers, station staff or shopkeepers do not know always where a particular company or building is located, even if you have the address written down.

When you are visiting someone's home for the first time, it is easier to meet at the local station. When arranging to meet, remember that there are usually two or more station exits.

6 宇田川町方面
しぶちか経由
西武百貨店
渋谷パルコ
渋谷区役所
渋谷公会堂
NHK放送センター

7a 神南方面
109-②
丸井

8 ハチ公方面
しぶちか経由
東急百貨店東横店

1 This sign gives information about **eki no deguchi** (station exits). You are going to the Parco Department Store. What number exit should you take? (To help you, first work out how to write **paruko** in **katakana**. See the **katakana** chart on pages 78–79.)

Traveling around

Shinkansen

Densha (trains) in Japan are run by private operators. The largest rail network is Japan Railways which runs the world-famous **shinkansen**, nicknamed 'the bullet train' because it is very fast.

The original **shinkansen** route runs west from **Tōkyō** to **Kyōto**, **Hiroshima** and, through the **Shimonoseki** Tunnel, down to **Hakata** in the north of **Kyūshū**. Traveling at speeds up to 240 kilometers per hour (150 miles per hour), the fast **hikari** (light) service makes the 1,170-kilometer (726-mile) journey to **Hakata** in just over 6½ hours. The slower trains, which make additional stops, are called **kodama** (echo).

The two other **shinkansen** routes run from **Tōkyō** up the east coast and across to the west coast.

The **shinkansen** system is fully computerized. Trains leave exactly on time. There is one about every 15 minutes to the major cities. On the platform, the trains always stop in exactly the same place, so passengers know where to wait in line for the compartment where their seats are.

You can buy a ticket for the **shinkansen** at the **midori no madoguchi** (green window) at major Japan Railways stations. You need a **jōshaken** (regular ticket) and an extra **shinkansen** ticket, either **jiyūseki** (unreserved seat) or **shiteiseki** (reserved seat). A single ticket is **katamichi** and a return, **ōfuku**.

Densha

As well as the **shinkansen**, there are other kinds of **densha** (trains):

futsū	local train that stops at each station
kyūkō	an express that stops only at certain places between two larger towns
tokkyū	an express that runs direct between two large towns

The most comfortable way to travel by train is in a **guriin sha** (green car) on **kyūkō**, **tōkkyu** and **shinkansen** trains. Passengers in **guriin sha** have a more comfortable seat and a footrest.

For numbers from 100 to 9,999 use the following words. Also see page 20.

100	百	hyaku	1,000	千	sen	
200	二百	ni-hyaku	2,000	二千	ni-sen	
300	三百	san-byaku	3,000	三千	san-zen	
400	四百	yon-hyaku	4,000	四千	yon-sen	
500	五百	go-hyaku	5,000	五千	go-sen	
600	六百	roppyaku	6,000	六千	roku-sen	
700	七百	nana-hyaku	7,000	七千	nana-sen	
800	八百	happyaku	8,000	八千	hassen	
900	九百	kyū-hyaku	9,000	九千	kyū-sen	

For example:
1,516 = **sen go-hyaku jū-roku**
8,951 = **hassen kyū-hyaku go-jū-ichi**
9,999 = **kyū-sen kyū-hyaku kyū-jū-kyū**

1 Write out the numbers given as an example above in **kanji** (characters).

☐ Try saying these numbers in Japanese:
a	2,345	**e**	3,667
b	9,876	**f**	1,088
c	603	**g**	7,200
d	4,711	**h**	599

Kyōto made

きょうとまでのじょうしゃけんと
しんかんせんのじゆうせきをください。
A ticket and a **shinkansen** supplement
to **Kyōto** please.

かたみちですか、おうふくですか。 One way or round trip?

かたみちです。 One way.

いくらですか。　　　二千三百四十円です。
How much is that?　　It's 2,340 yen.

☐ With a partner.
A wants to buy a round-trip **shinkansen** ticket to **Tōkyō**.
B is selling the ticket. It costs 3,490 yen.

Norimono

Other **norimono** (means of transport) round Japan include: **hikōki** (airoplanes), **chōkyoribasu** or **haiuei basu** (coaches) and **ferii** (ferries). Comfortable, air-conditioned long-distance buses with telephones are an inexpensive alternative to **densha** or **hikōki**.

Before **Honshū**, **Shikoku**, **Kyūshū** and **Hokkaidō** were linked by road and rail tunnels and bridges, people often traveled from one island to another by **ferii**.

Some **fune** (ships) visit a number of ports. One line goes from **Tōkyō** to **Kushiro** on **Hokkaidō**. On board are restaurants, bars and even **o furo** (Japanese baths).

The national airline, Japan Airlines, and five smaller airlines fly to 60 airports around the country. Most internal flights from Tōkyō leave from Haneda Airport. Narita is the airport for international flights.

In the street

Some **hyōshiki** (signs), such as road signs, are easy to understand because they are international. Other **hyōshiki** are place names that are written in **rōmaji** or give directions in English in the **dōri** (main streets) and tourist areas of cities such as **Tōkyō**, **Yokohama** and **Kyōto**.

The Japanese drive on the left. When crossing the road at **shingō** (traffic lights) where two streets intersect, look out for cars turning the corner toward you. They are only obliged to stop if pedestrians are crossing.

1 There is a sign for a **karaoke** bar with an arrow in it. Which way should you go? (See the **katakana** chart on pages 78–79.)

Kōban (small police kiosks) can be found near stations and even in quiet residential areas. As well as dealing with petty crime, keikan (the police) spend a lot of time giving directions, because Japanese street numbering is not always very logical.

When the word tōri is part of a street name it becomes dōri.

Roads and streets in Japan are often narrow, so there's not much room for parking. Before buying a jidōsha (car), drivers have to prove that they have a private parking space for it. People who take a chance and park in the street have to pay to get their jidōsha from the impound lot.

Jūsho

Jūsho (addresses) are listed by district and block number, rather than by street. In **Tōkyō**, there are 23 districts called **ku**. Each **ku** is made up of smaller areas, which in turn are subdivided into **chōme**. After that comes the block number and the building number.

Here is how a typical address is made up:

東京都	新宿区	下落合	3丁目	-21番	-22号
Tōkyō-to	Shinjuku-ku	Shimo Ochiai	San chōme	Ni-jū ichiban	Ni-jū-ni gō
CITY or PREFECTURE	DISTRICT	AREA	CHŌME	BLOCK NUMBER	BUILDING NUMBER

ゴミ容器集積所

ゴミの収集日		
普通ゴミ 台所ゴミ(生ゴミ)・紙くず など	月	水 金
分別ゴミ プラスチック・ゴム・皮革 金属・ガラス・セトモノ 筒型乾電池 など	木	
粗大ゴミ ゴミ容器に入らない 大きなゴミ	申込み制です 電話等で清掃事務所にご連絡ください。お宅まで収集に伺いますので、ここには出さないでください。	

台所ゴミは水をよく切って出してください。
ゴミ容器には必ずフタと名前を、いつも清潔に、収集が終ったらすぐ引取ってください。

ゴミはきちんと分別して出しましょう

東京都 豊島 清掃事務所☎(984) 9681

ゴミの集積所につき駐車はご遠慮ください

Gomi (refuse) is removed from special collection points. People have to take bags of refuse to the nearest collection point, usually just a short distance away.

Look at the sign. There are three days a week on which **gomi** that can be burned is collected. These days are shown in the first section with three trash can symbols.

[2] Say which days of the week this type of refuse is collected in Japanese and English. (See the **kanji** (characters) for the days of the week on page 28.)

Ichiba (street markets), like this fish market, have a lively atmosphere. Special Sunday markets are good places for bargains in clothes and household goods. Bright **chōchin** (lanterns) decorate the streets, accompanied by the cries of street traders and traditional music and the smell of **yakitori** (grilled chicken pieces on a stick).

Kōen de

On **shūmatsu** (weekends), **kōen** (parks) are crowded with families. Since most families do not have gardens at home and fathers do not always see much of their children during the week, it is a good chance to go out together for a stroll.

As well as open spaces **Ueno Kōen** in **Tōkyō** (right) offers visitors five museums, including the National Museum and the Tokyo Metropolitan Art Museum, and a zoo.

The area name, **chōme** and block number are shown on buildings or electricity pylons. To find an address, however, you still have to know in which direction the block numbers run. In some blocks, the buildings are numbered according to when they were built.

Look at the photo on the left.
[3] Read the **hiragana** down the right-hand side of the sign to find the area name. (See the **hiragana** chart on pages 78–79.)
[4] What is the number of the **chōme**? (See the **kanji** for numbers on pages 20–21.)
[5] Work out the numbers of these **chōme**. (See pages 20–21.)

a 五丁目   b 三丁目

Somewhere to stay

Ryokan to minshuku

Staying in a **ryokan** (Japanese-style hotel) in the countryside is one way to experience the traditional Japanese way of life.

On arrival, guests are greeted by a maid who shows them to their rooms. Later, she serves food and, after dinner, lays out the **futon**, traditional Japanese-style bedding, and says **o yasuminasai** (good night) to the guests. This doesn't mean guests are expected to go to sleep at 8 p.m., just that they won't be disturbed until the next morning.

There are about 2,000 **ryokan** in Japan. A room at a **ryokan** may be more expensive than a western-style hotel, but the price includes dinner and Japanese-style breakfast.

◀ At about 6 p.m., **yūshoku** (dinner) is served, usually in the room. People take a relaxing **o-furo** (hot bath) before (or after) **yūshoku**, and put on comfortable **yukata** (cotton **kimono**-style robes).

◀ All **ryokan** rooms have **tatami** matting on the floor. They are plainly furnished with a **tēburu** (table) with cushions around it and a **tokonoma**, an alcove for a plant or a picture. One concession to modern life is **terebi** (television). Many rooms also have a view over a small, but beautifully laid-out garden.

A **minshuku** is much less formal and less expensive than a **ryokan**. It is a sort of Japanese-style bed and breakfast. **Asagohan** (breakfast) is taken with the family (**yūshoku**, too, if it is available). Guests usually provide their own **yukata**, towel and soap. They lay out the **futon** themselves, and put it away in the closet in the morning.

Hoteru

◀ **Hoteru** are western-style hotels found in the big cities. Many are first-class hotels with a selection of restaurants and a swimming pool.

Note that the electrical current operates at 100 volts, and visitors would have to use an adaptor for electrical equipment.

Business Hotel Nishiik
ビジネスホテ
西池
☎ 971-6234·053

Heya ni

Here are some things you may find in your **hoteru no heya** (hotel room):

terebi	テレビ	television
rajio	ラジオ	radio
denwa	でんわ	telephone
basu	バス	western-style bath
shawā	シャワー	shower

Potto ポット

A **futon** is a thick cotton mattress laid out on **tatami** matting (on the floor). It has a quilt (with a cover) on top.

— 日本語 —

To ask about which items are in your **heya** (room), say. . .

Heya ni terebi ga arimasu ka?
へやにテレビがありますか。
Is there a television in the room?

If there is, you will hear. . .

> *Hai, arimasu.*

If there is not, you will hear. . .

> *Iie, arimasen.*

If you want to explain that something is missing, say. . .

Heya ni rajio ga arimasen.
へやにラジオがありません。
There's no radio in the room.

□ Explain at the **furonto** (reception, literally 'front' from 'front desk') that you don't have the following things in your room:

oyu	おゆ	hot water
tii baggu	ティーバッグ	tea bags
toiretto pēpā	トイレットペーパー	toilet paper
sekken	せっけん	soap
basu taoru	バスタオル	bath towel

□ Work with a partner.
Ask your partner if he or she has any of these things in his or her bedroom:
a a desk
b a telephone
c a television
d a bath towel

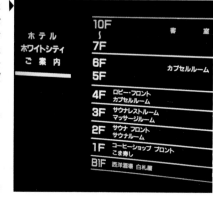

Anata no heya ni denwa ga arimasu ka?

Jinesu hoteru (business hotels) offer rooms at less than half the price of the top **hoteru**. 'Room service' comes from a vending machine. In many rooms there is a **potto** (thermos flask) so guests can make themselves tea.

The **kapuseru hoteru** (capsule hotel) is a unique Japanese invention. A space just large enough for a bed and small television is provided. **Kapuseru hoteru** are popular with **sarariiman** (male office workers) who have missed the last train home and need somewhere inexpensive to sleep.

1 At the White City Hotel work out to which floor you would go:
a for something to eat and drink.
b to ask for an inexpensive room.
c for a sauna and massage.
(See the **katakana** chart on pages 78–79.)

ホテル	10F
ホワイトシティ	〜 客室
ご案内	7F
	6F カプセルルーム
	5F
	4F ロビー・フロント カプセルルーム
	3F サウナレストルーム マッサージルーム
	2F サウナ フロント サウナルーム
	1F コーヒーショップ フロント こま寿し
	B1F 西洋酒場 白札屋

Money to spend

O kane

The **o kane** (money) used in Japan is the yen. The notes are 1,000, 5,000 and 10,000 yen. One-, five-, 10-, 50-, 100-, and 500-yen coins are in circulation.

Sen en 1,000 円

Go-sen en 5,000 円

Ichi-man en 10,000 円

There are two ways of indicating **yen**: one is ¥ and the other is the **kanji** (character) 円. This **kanji** is used because it can be read as **en**, meaning 'yen'. It is used for prices in shops. The actual meaning of the **kanji** is 'circle'.

 How much is 5,000 yen worth in dollars? Find out what the yen exchange rate is to the dollar from a newspaper or a bank.

On the 10,000-yen note the usual **kanji** for 'one' — does not appear. Instead a special **kanji** is used. On official documents any numbers that could be altered by adding extra strokes are replaced by special **kanji** that cannot be altered.

 Hyaku en 100 円

 Go-jū en 50 円

Jū en 10 円

Kaimono

Irasshaimase.

Kaimono (shopping) is a favorite pastime of many Japanese. The large **depāto** (department stores) are open from about 10 a.m. to 7 p.m. six days a week, including Sundays. The best known ones include **Seibu** and **Mitsukoshi**. They stock selections of Japanese and imported goods.

Japanese products, especially electrical goods, are of excellent quality. Famous name brands from abroad are also very popular, especially fashion items, cosmetics and whisky.

A three per cent sales tax is usually added to the prices marked on items in shops.

*You are often welcomed when you walk into a shop, a bank or a restaurant. In **depāto** an erebētā gāru ('elevator girl' or female operator) bows to customers as they enter the lift.*

Depāto

Up to 9,999 numbers are counted in **sen** (thousands), **hyaku** (hundreds) and **jū** (tens). (See pages 20–21 and 42–43.)

For numbers above 10,000 the Japanese use **man**, a unit of 10,000.

10,000	一万	ichi-man
20,000	二万	ni-man
30,000	三万	san-man
40,000	四万	yon-man
50,000	五万	go-man
60,000	六万	roku-man
70,000	七万	nana-man
80,000	八万	hachi-man
90,000	九万	kyū-man
100,000	十万	jū-man

For example:
15,210 =	ichi-man go-sen ni-hyaku jū
20,000 =	ni-man
100,000 =	jū-man
147,598 =	jū-yon-man nana-sen go-hyaku kyū-jū hachi.
1,000,000 =	hyaku-man

☐ Practice saying these numbers in Japanese.

a	28,983	**e**	1,000,789
b	192,117	**f**	66,442
c	567,100	**g**	87,104
d	10,099	**h**	2,467,921

1 Using the **kanji** given on this page, as well as on pages 20–21 and 42–43, write out the numbers above in **kanji**.

Sometimes, numbers are written as combinations of **kanji** and figures. Look at the examples below.

a 10万円

b 97万1,000円

c 八五〇〇円

2 Write out the amount of each price above in **rōmaji**.

Ginkō

Since it can be difficult to pay with travelers' checks in shops and hotels, make sure to carry enough money in yen. (Generally, Japan is a safe place.)

To change money at the **ginkō** (bank) customers put their travelers' checks into a plastic tray at the counter and wait for their names to be called.

At busy times there may be confusion if there are two Japanese customers have a common surname such as **Tanaka** or **Suzuki**.

Ginkō are open from 9 a.m. to 3 p.m. Monday to Friday.

*Traditionally, many smaller **mise** (shops) are family-run. They stay open until about 8 p.m. in the large cities. This **mise** sells **kudamono** (fruit).*

*The appearance of 24-hour **konbiniensu sutoa** ('convenience stores') in local neighborhoods has put pressure on more traditional shops to stay open later.*

*If you're too late for the shops, try a vending machine. Street vending machines sell cold drinks, cans of soup already heated, ice cubes or even alcohol and **manga** (comic books).*

Japan has over five million vending machines (that is one for every 24 people) which is the highest number per person in the world.

B Are vending machines used much in your country?

Something to buy

O miyage

When the Japanese go on trips, even for just an overnight stay, they buy **o miyage**. These are small gifts to offer to relatives, friends or co-workers as souvenirs.

Typical **o miyage** might be local **okashi** (sweets) such as **manjū** which are filled with sweet bean paste. Young people like to buy **kii horudā** (key rings), **magu kappu** (coffee mugs), **kukkii** (biscuits) and **terehon kādo** (telephone cards) with local views.

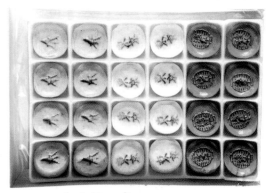

Manjū まんじゅう

(A) What **o miyage** would you choose as a souvenir of your country for a Japanese visitor?

*Local supermarkets sell prettily-patterned **kyūsu** (teapots) and **yuno-michawan** (cups) for drinking **o cha** (Japanese tea). A packet of **o cha** is another interesting reminder of Japan.*

*An unusual **o miyage** from Japan—an individual piece of **sush** in plastic! This shop sells plastic models of food to restaurants. You could also buy a **noren**. This is the curtain that hangs over the entrances to restaurants and shops.*

日本語

When you go to do some **kaimono** (shopping), you may need to ask about the opening hours of a **mise** (shop). Look at the **Nihongo** section on page 24 which gives the time in Japanese.

Nan-ji ni akimasu ka?
なん時にあきますか。
What time do you open?

Jū-ji ni akimasu.
十時にあきます。
We open at ten o'clock.

Nan-ji ni shimarimasu ka?
なん時にしまりますか。
What time do you close?

Shichi-ji ni shimarimasu.
七時にしまります。
We close at seven o'clock.

Flower Shop こころ
平日 AM 10:00~PM 6:00
休日 PM 12:00~PM 6:00

1 In Japanese, say what time this flower shop closes.

(B) In Japanese, say what time the supermarket nearest to where you live opens.

Mingeihin

The tradition of high quality **mingeihin** (handicrafts) goes back many centuries. Even apparently simple items, such as paper or pottery, are made with such skill and care that they become almost works of art.

Setomono: Ceramics are known as **setomono**. The word comes from **Seto**, a city in the **Chūbu** region famous for its ceramics for more than 600 years.

Further south in **Kyūshū**, Korean potters were brought to Japan to teach their skills in pottery to the local people.

Shikki (Lacquerware) is made by building up layers of paint and polishing it. Plain **shikki**, such as bowls and trays, are used every day, although plastic imitations of **shikki** are also very common. The most famous place for **shikki** is **Wajima**, not far from **Kanazawa**.

Sensu: Hand-painted silk and paper folding fans are now used mainly for decoration. They are also used in traditional dances and **nō** and **kabuki** plays. **Sensu** are decorated with words or poems written in **kanji** (characters) and with patterns.

Ningyō: Japanese people have always been interested in **ningyō** (dolls). **Kokeshi** are painted wooden dolls without arms or legs. They come originally from the northeast of Japan.

Shikki しっき

Setomono ya せとものや

Kokeshi こけし

Daruma are dolls made of papier mâché or wood. The eyes are not painted in. People make a wish and paint one eye on the **daruma**. If they get their wish, they paint in the other eye.

日本語

When you are in a shop and you want to look at something, you can ask:

...o misete kudasai.
...をみせてください。
Please show me...

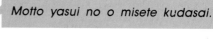

Ano sensu o misete kudasai.

Motto yasui no o misete kudasai.

2 What item does the customer want to look at?
3 Does the customer want to pay this price?

ano ningyō	あのにんぎょう	that doll
ano hashi	あのはし	those chopsticks
are	あれ	that (thing)
motto chiisai no	もっとちいさいの	a smaller one
motto ōkii no	もっとおおきいの	a bigger one
motto yasui no	もっとやすいの	a cheaper one

☐ Practice asking a shop assistant to show you:
  a that tea cup   **c** that shop curtain
  b those sweets   **d** that (thing)

Eating out

Nihon no ryōri

In **Nihon no ryōri** (Japanese cooking), the freshest possible fish, meat and vegetables should be used. Presentation also plays a part. Even a simple meal is carefully arranged.

Gohan (rice) or noodles appears in almost all Japanese meals. The important part still played by fish, seafood and seaweed emphasizes Japan's links with the sea. It was only in the 19th century that the Japanese started to eat meat in any quantity.

Some of the more popular food items available are described in this section. The **hiragana** or **kanji** (character) for each dish is shown it would appear on a menu.

The versatile soybean appears in many forms, including **tōfu** *(high-protein bean curd). It is fermented to make* **shōyu** *(soy sauce) for seasoning and* **miso** *paste used for making* **miso shiru** *(miso soup).*

Sushi: The most common kind is **nigiri zushi**, a small block of vinegared rice with a dab of green **wasabi**, a powerful horseradish paste, and a slice of **sashimi** (raw fish), seafood or omelette on top. Another kind of **sushi** contains fish or vegetables in the middle of the rice. A strip of **nori** (dried black seaweed) is wrapped around the rice.

The way of eating **sushi** is to pour a little **shōyu** into a small saucer and dip the **sushi** in.

Look out for the cheaper **sushi-ya** *(sushi restaurants) where the* **sushi** *circulates on a mini conveyor belt. You help yourself and pay according to the number of dishes you have taken.*

Resutoran

The top floors of **depāto** (department stores) have a variety of **resutoran** (restaurants). The more expensive **resutoran** are higher up. Below are inexpensive **famirii resutoran** (family restaurants) which serve Japanese and western food. Chinese food is also inexpensive and very popular. Snack food can be sampled in the **depāto** basement.

Gaikoku no ryōri (foreign cooking) includes Italian, French and American food. A **naifu** (knife) and **fōku** (fork) are brought for eating western-style food.

Resutoran display models of food, so customers know exactly what they are getting! This originated in the 19th century when **resutoran** started serving western-style food that many Japanese had never seen before.

These models are outside a **kissaten**, *a café, where* **kōhii** *(coffee), light snacks and desserts are served.*

天ぷらおねがいします。
May I have some **tempura**, please

すきやき **Sukiyaki:** At the table, thin slices of beef, **tōfu**, spring onions and other vegetables are simmered in a sauce of **shōyu** and **sake**. Before being eaten, the meat or vegetables are dipped into beaten raw egg. **Sukiyaki** is a dish that is usually eaten at home.

*The ingredients for **sukiyaki***

焼肉 **Yakiniku:** The meat is cooked on a grill in the middle of the table, then dipped into a spicy sauce. Squid and vegetables may also be grilled in the same way. There are tasty side dishes, such as **kimuchi** (pickled white cabbage with red chili powder) and **namuru** with spinach, bean sprouts and radish.

Some other **Nihon no ryōri:**

天ぷら **Tempura:** Prawns, fish and vegetables are deep-fried in batter, then dipped in **tentsuyu**, a sauce of **shōyu**, **sake** and grated radish.

うなぎ **Unagi:** The older generation, in particular, enjoys slices of eel which are charcoal-broiled in **tare** sauce. **Una don** (eel on rice) makes a tasty snack.

とんかつ **Ton katsu:** A deep-fried breadcrumbed pork cutlet is served with a brown sauce and raw shredded cabbage.

釜めし **Kamameshi:** This is rice steamed in a pot with meat or seafood.

お好み焼 **Okonomiyaki:** A type of pancake is made with eggs and pork, chicken, shrimp or vegetables. It is usually cooked at the table.

鍋物 **Nabemono:** This is literally 'one-pot cooking'. At the table, vegetables, fish (salmon or cod), oysters or meat are cooked in a large pot of boiling stock.

日本語

おちゃください。
Some tea, please.

おかんじょうおねがいします。
May I have the check, please?

Nomimono

If you want **nomimono** (something to drink), try:

O cha: Green tea, drunk without milk or sugar. In most restaurants, it is served free with food.

Kō cha: Black tea, served with lemon or milk.

Kōhii: Usually fresh coffee.

O sake: Traditional rice wine, served warm in a small porcelain flask. When with other people, *never* serve yourself. Wait for another person to serve you.

O mizu: A glass of water. (The usual word for 'cold water' is **mizu**.)

Biiru: Since the 19th century, the Japanese have been making beer.'

Jūsu: Soft drink.

Kōra: Cola.

The Japanese for 'Cheers' is **kampai!**

Fast food

Soba to udon to rāmen

*Slurping noodles is not considered rude. It can be a way of showing that the food is **oishii** (delicious). At the end of a meal, it is polite to say **Gochisōsama deshita** to the waiter or the person who prepared the food. It means literally 'it was an honorable feast'.*

Noodles are typical Japanese fast food. The main types are **soba** (buckwheat noodles in broth) or **udon** (white-flour noodles in broth). A winter favorite, **nabeyaki udon**, has shrimps, egg and vegetables. **Zaru soba**, cold noodles with dried **nori** on top and served with a sauce, is often eaten in summer. **Shichimi** seasoning adds spice to the hot dishes.

Restaurants serving **soba** also serve **donburi**, a dish of meat or chicken (sometimes with egg, too) a helping of rice and flavored with **shōyu** (soy sauce).

Rāmen are Chinese-style egg noodles in a chicken or pork broth. **Tanmen** are noodles served with vegetables and **chāshūmen** is with roast pork.

*If you want something to take out, say **mochikaerimasu** or **teiku auto**. For those too busy to go out for lunch, many **soba-ya** (noodle shops) deliver orders by motorcycle.*

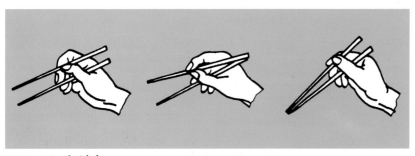

O hashi おはし

◀ *Japanese **o hashi** (chopsticks) are generally shorter than Chinese chopsticks. In **resutoran**, disposable wooden chopsticks are used. They come partially split and have to be pulled apart. Some people rub them together to make sure there are no splinters.*

*Before you start to eat, it is the custom to say **Itadakimasu** to the people you are with.*

Chūshoku

Oishii bentō desu ne?

For **chūshoku** (lunch), many working people have a **bentō** (a boxed lunch) brought from home or bought at a **bentō** shop. The box has separate sections for rice (with an **umeboshi**, or pickled plum, on top), salad, vegetables and either chicken, meat or fish.

For hot food at lunchtime, most **resutoran** ▶ (restaurants) offer set menus. **Teishoku** is usually a set meal of Japanese or Chinese food including **miso** soup, a main dish, rice, salad and pickles. A **setto menyū** is usually western-style food.

Hanbāgā

Hanbāgā resutoran (hamburger restaurants) and other fast food outlets are found everywhere. Students like to go there after school, and they are popular with families on Sundays.

The big American hanbāgā chains and their Japanese counterparts are much the same as anywhere else. Some concessions to local taste are teriyaki bāgā (burgers flavored with a sauce of shōyu and other ingredients) and tako sarada (octopus salad).

Items on the menu are written in katakana. They are always pronounced the Japanese way.

1 Work out how to write hanbāgā in katakana. Use the chart on page 79 to help you.

☐ Look at the following menu items written in katakana. Practice reading them aloud. Can you work out what they are in English?

a チーズバーガー   d コーヒー
b フィッシュバーガー   e オレンジジュース
c フライドポテト   f バニラシェイク

2 Look at the picture of a teriyaki bāgā with fries and a green salad. Which of the three descriptions in katakana below goes with the picture?

a ダブルバーガー

    フライドポテト　コーラ

b テリヤキバーガー

    フライドポテト　コーヒー

c テリヤキバーガー

    フライドポテト　グリーンサラダ

── 日本語 ──

When ordering food in a fast food resutoran, use these special numbers:

hitotsu	one	muttsu	six
futatsu	two	nanatsu	seven
mittsu	three	yattsu	eight
yottsu	four	kokonotsu	nine
itsutsu	five	tō	ten

For example:

Hanbāgā o futatsu kudasai.
ハンバーガーをふたつください。
Two hamburgers, please.

Teriyaki bāgā o hitotsu to orenji jūsu o mittsu kudasai.
テリヤキバーガーをひとつとオレンジジュース
をみっつください。
One teriyaki burger and three orange juices, please.

☐ How would you ask for these items in a hanbāgā resutoran?
a Three fishburgers.
b A hamburger and a coffee.
c Two cheeseburgers and three vanilla shakes.
d Six teriyaki burgers and four octopus salads.
e Eight hamburgers and seven portions of fries.

Fisshyu bāgā...

Keeping in touch

E hagaki

Japanese people do not usually send **e hagaki** (picture post-cards) when they are on holiday. Postcards with views of Japan are sold at the larger hotels where foreign visitors stay or at major tourist sites. **Depāto** (departments stores) also stock postcards.

O **shōgatsu** (New Year) is the time for sending cards. Everyone sends them—friends, colleagues, business contacts. **Nengajō** are special New Year cards which are available at post offices. They have numbers printed on them which go into a prize draw.

*The address on this card for **O shōgatsu** is written from top to bottom and goes from right to left. Because Japanese is often written from top to bottom, paper for writing **tegami** (letters) has vertical lines.*

Yūbin kyoku

Kitte (stamps) can be bought at the **yūbin kyoku** (post office) and in some small shops. **Tegami** and **e hagaki** which are larger than standard size may be charged at a higher rate.

If you are not sure how much the postage will cost, hand your cards or letters to the postal clerk. Say **Onegaishimasu** and the clerk will sort things out for you. Airmail is **kōkūbin**.

*Left: This sign can be seen outside all **yūbin kyoku** (post offices) and also small shops that sell stamps.*
*Right: This is a **posuto** (post box).*

--- 日本語 ---

When buying **kitte**, use the numbers, **ichi**, **ni**, **san**, **shi**, etc., which you will find on pages 20–21 and 42–43. The number is followed by **mai**, the counting word for flat objects.

Kore wa Amerika made ikura desu ka?

Hyaku en desu.

Hyaku en no kitte o rokumai kudasai.

これはアメリカまで
いくらですか。
How much is it to send this to America?

百えんです。
100 yen.

百えんのきってを
ろくまいください。
Please give me six 100-yen stamps.

☐ Practice asking for stamps in Japanese. First say the value of the stamp in Japanese. Then ask for the number of stamps of that value that you want.

a Five 41-yen stamps
b Nine 62-yen stamps
c Six 120-yen stamps
d Twenty 10-yen stamps

Denwa

There are **denwa** (telephones) everywhere in Japan—in **kissaten** (cafés), on train station platforms, in side streets. Pay-phones—red phones take only 10-yen pieces and the yellow ones take 10- and 100-yen pieces—are gradually being replaced by green phones which take **terehon kādo** (phone cards). Some green phones also take coins.

Terehon kādo, costing from 500 yen up, can be bought in shops or from the machines located near the telephones themselves.

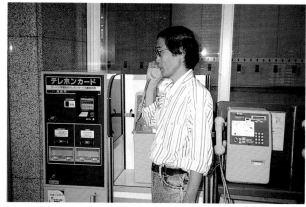

Terehon kādo no denwa
テレホンカードのでんわ。

At extra cost, **terehon kādo** with photos of pop singers are available. Personalized **kādo** are given away by companies as promotions. At weddings, guests are sometimes given **terehōn kādo** with the names of the happy couple on them.

Limited edition or rarer **terehon kādo** have become collectors' items. They are never used, because they would be perforated when a call is made.

USA: Country code: **1**
New York area code: **212**
Number: **123-4567**

Dial: **001-1-212-123-4567**

Making a call **kaigai ni** (overseas) can be done by direct-dialing from special green pay phones marked 'International Telephone' in English and **katakana**.

--- 日本語 ---

When you give a **denwa bangō** (telephone number) in Japanese, the word **no** indicates a hyphen or the end of a group of numbers. The word for '0' is **maru**. (See page 20 for numbers from one to nine.)

For example: **3952-3109** is **san-kyū-go-ni no san-ichi-maru-kyū**.

☐ With a partner.
Ask your partner to tell you his or her phone number in Japanese.

Anata no denwa bangō wa nan ban desu ka?

Watashi no denwa bangō wa . . .

☐ Look at the dialing instructions above for phoning your country. If you had to tell someone in Japanese what numbers to dial for your home, how would you say it?

Remember to include: the country code, the area code, your telephone number.

Moshi moshi.

Hai, imasu. Chotto matte kudasai.

Moshi moshi. Hashimoto desu. Tanaka-san irasshaimasu ka?

1 Read through the telephone conversation. In Japanese, how would you say the following phrases:
  a Just a moment, please.
  b Is Mr. **Suzuki** there?
  c Hello. (Only used for the phone.)
  d This is Miss **Takano**.
  e Yes, he is (here).

Family life

Kazoku

The idea of **kazoku** (the family) is very strong in Japan. The husband and the wife have clearly defined roles. The husband works to provide financial security for the family. In return, his wife looks after the house. She controls the family budget and makes important decisions affecting the family. Although the husband is treated as the head of the house, his wife may be the one who decides how much pocket money he may have from his salary.

As husbands come home from work late in the evening, family members often lead separate lives on weekdays, with their own interests and their own friends. Because a husband and wife are not used to spending much time together, when they retire things can become difficult. Although divorces are still rare in Japan, there are perhaps more among retired people than in other countries.

*About a quarter of Japanese people still have **miai kekkon** (arranged marriages) where a man and a woman are formally introduced by a person known to both families. Someone looking for a partner may meet several people before making a decision about whom to marry.*

Couples who marry for love often meet their partners at college or through work.

*In a typical Japanese **kazoku**, there are two or three children. Younger children are expected to be respectful to their elder brothers and sisters.*

*It is generally still the custom for older people to live with one of their children. Elderly relatives who live outside the big cities are usually visited during **O bon** and **O shōgatsu** (New Year).*

*Some older people whose children have left small towns or the countryside to live in **Tōkyō** or **Ōsaka** feel isolated.*

*Many more women are taking up careers. There were always many female teachers and nurses, but now more women are becoming school principals, executive officers and even politicians. **Takako Doi** (right) became the leader of the Japan Socialist Party for a few years, although she is still an exception in male-dominated Japan.*

In Japanese, people use one set of words to talk *about* members of their own families and a more polite set of words to talk *to* those same family members or to talk *about* other people's families.

For example, 'my mother' would be **haha**. 'Mother' or someone else's mother would be **okāsan**.

sofu my grandfather
ojiisan grandfather (polite)

sobo my grandmother
obāsan grandmother (polite)

chichi my father
otōsan father (polite)

haha my mother
okāsan mother (polite)

musume my daughter
ojōsan daughter (polite)

musuko my son
botchan son (polite)

(A) Make up a **keizu** (family ...
family including your g...
your parents and your b...
sisters. For each person wr...
  a the name
  b what relation they are to you. For example, write **sofu** for your grandfather or **imōto** for your younger sister.

☐ With a partner.
Keep the **keizu** for your family in front of you, but out of sight of your partner. Now ask your partner the names of these members of his or her family.
  a grandmother
  b father
  c mother
  d grandfather
Your partner can ask you the same questions. You can check if you have the correct information by looking at your partner's **keizu**.

Ojiisan no namae wa nan desu ka?

Sofu no namae wa . . . desu.

Among brothers and sisters there are special words for 'older sister' or 'younger brother'. In parentheses are the words used for talking to someone in your family or about someone else's family.

ani
(oniisan)
elder brother

ane
(onēsan)
elder sister

otōto
(otōto san)
younger brother

imōto
(imōto san)
younger sister

(B) Try to answer these questions about your brothers and sisters in Japanese.
  a Otōto san no namae wa nan desu ka?
  b Onēsan no namae wa nan desu ka?

If you do not have any brothers or sisters, you can explain you are an only child:

Hitorikko desu.

side a Japanese house

Nihon no ie

Traditional **ie** (houses) in Japan are built from wood. Older style houses can still be seen, especially in country areas. The space inside the house is divided into rooms by **fusuma**, paper partitions that slide open. The floors are covered in **tatami**, a kind of straw matting.

The size of a room is measured according to the number of **tatami** mats that fit into it. A regular **tatami** mat is 1.80 meters (5.9 feet) by 90 centimeters (2.95 feet). A living room is usually a **hachi-jō** (eight-mat room). A bedroom might be the size of 4.5 **tatami** mats.

A very large traditional house that is now open to the public.

*The original Japanese idea is to leave rooms very simple without much furniture. In the main sitting room there is a low table but no chairs because people sit on cushions. There is a **tokonoma** (alcove) with a scroll or an elegant flower arrangement.*

*Any **heya** (room) can easily be changed into a bedroom by moving the furniture to one side and laying out **futon**. (See page 47.)*

*Winters can be very cold in Japan. A room is often only heated when people are using it. A **kotatsu** is a kind of table with a heater underneath. A warm **futon** covers the edge of the table and people put their legs underneath to keep warm.*

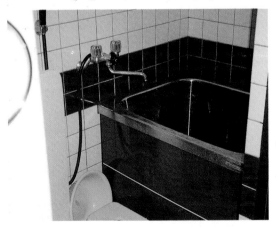

Although older houses are ▶ admired for their style, many families now live in concrete houses or buildings which have more modern conveniences. A typical home is a '4LDK'— four rooms plus a living room, a dining-kitchen area, a small bathroom and a toilet.

◀ Japanese people like to relax in **o furo**, the deep, square Japanese-style baths. The custom is first to wash and rinse off, then get into the **o furo** for a long soak in hot water.

*As space is limited in big cities, the carpeted, western-style rooms of modern Japanese homes may look a little crowded. The sitting room may have a sofa, a bookcase, a coffee table, a stereo, a television and video recorder. One or two of the rooms might have **tatami** matting. Bedrooms may have **beddo** (beds) rather than **futon**.*

(A) What is the difference between a Japanese house and your home? Look for some differences:

a between a traditional Japanese house and the house where you live.

b between a modern Japanese house and the house where you live.

——— 日本語 ———

ie	いえ	house
heya	へや	room (general word)
ima	いま	sitting room
daidokoro	だいどころ	kitchen
toire	トイレ	toilet
yokushitsu	よくしつ	bathroom
shosai	しょさい	study
shinshitsu	しんしつ	bedroom
oshiire	おしいれ	closet
kaidan	かいだん	stairs
beranda	ベランダ	veranda
genkan	げんかん	entrance

1 Look at these two lists of words. Match the things on the left with the room where you might expect to find them in a house.

a	o furo	**1**	toire
b	sofā	**2**	ima
c	futon	**3**	daidokoro
d	reizōko (fridge)	**4**	shosai
e	tsukue (desk)	**5**	shinshitsu
f	toiretto pēpā	**6**	yokushitsu

(B) Draw a plan of the place where you live. Label the rooms with their Japanese names.

Dōzo agatte kudasai

*A visitor to the house is usually greeted with the words **Dōzo agatte kudasai**, which means 'Please come up.' Always bring a cake, some chocolates or cookies if you are invited to dinner.*

The Japanese generally regard their houses as too humble to invite guests to, but house-warming parties are sometimes held. When you arrive in a Japanese home, the first thing you see is a row of slippers. Everyone changes into slippers at the **genkan** (entrance). The slippers must be taken off before entering any **tatami** room.

Here is a plan of the **heya** in a typical family house:

yokushitsu	daidokoro	toire	shosai
			genkan
heya	ima		heya

oshiire	kaidan	toire	oshiire
shinshitsu			shinshitsu
			shinshitsu
	beranda		

eeping fit

Sumō

Sumō wrestling is the national sport and Japan's oldest, too. The wrestlers weigh up to 200 kilos (440 pounds). Before a bout they stare at each other, squat, stamp around and throw salt into the ring as part of the ritual.

The actual bout may only last a few seconds. The contest is over when one of the wrestlers is pushed out of the ring, or if any part of his body (except his feet) touches the ground.

A lot of training and skill is required to be a **sumō** wrestler. Agility and balance are as important as strength. Only a very few wrestlers can become **yokozuna**, the top-ranking wrestlers.

*All **sumō** wrestlers have professional names. One of the most popular **yokozuna** champions ever was **Chiyonofuji** who retired in 1991. His names means 'Eternal Mount Fuji.'*

*Wrestlers eat a lot of **chanko nabe**, a stew of meat, fish, vegetables and spices. This helps them to gain weight.*

Budō

Budō are martial arts. They are closely related to the **Zen** philosophy and are concerned with spiritual and mental development as well as self-defense.

Jūdō: (This literally means 'the gentle way.') The popularity of **jūdō** has spread all over the world since it was first featured in the Olympic Games held in **Tōkyō** in 1964.

Various holds and throws enable the unarmed person to protect himself or herself by using his or her opponent's strength to his or her own advantage.

Karate: ('The empty hand') This martial art developed in China over a thousand years ago and came to Japan by way of **Okinawa**. As well as the hands, the feet, elbows and head are used for sudden, precise blows on an opponent's body.

Supōtsu

*The most popular participation sport is **gorufu** (golf). About a third of male office workers over 40 belong to a club.*

*Although there are over 1,500 golf courses, it can cost up to 50 million **yen** to join a well-known club! Even playing a game is very expensive. Instead, many people have to settle for an hour or two at one of the (sometimes multi-story) driving ranges above.*

The **supōtsu** of **yakyū** (baseball) was introduced to Japan from the United States in 1873. The top university and high school teams draw big crowds. Twelve professional teams play in the two leagues (Central and Pacific). They have names such as the **Yomiuri** Giants and the **Seibu** Lions.

Tenisu (tennis) is a fashionable sport and young people like to wear designer sports wear when they play. Central **Honshū** and **Hokkaidō** have winter resorts for **sukii** (skiing). City dwellers, confined to their desks during the week, work out at the gym on weekends. Retired people go **jogingu** (jogging) in the park early in the morning.

Kendō, or 'the way of the sword,' is a type of fencing which was practiced by the *samurai* warriors. The protective clothing and bamboo staffs used today were introduced about 200 years ago.

Other traditional sports which have become popular again in recent years are **kyūdō** (archery), and **aikidō**, the philosophy and techniques of which are something like **jūdō**.

Sadaharu Ō had hit a world-record 868 home runs, when he retired in 1980.

─────── 日本語 ───────

These **supōtsu** are also very popular in Japan:

suiei	すいえい	swimming
sāfin	サーフィン	surfing
futtobōru	フットボール	football
sakkā	サッカー	soccer
badominton	バドミントン	badminton
basukettobōru	バスケットボール	basketball
barēbōru	バレーボール	volleyball
bōringu	ボーリング	bowling

You may want to talk about **supōtsu** that you like.

Tenisu ga suki desu ka?

Hai, suki desu.

Iie, suki dewa arimasen.

テニスがすきですか。
Do you like tennis?

はい、すきです。　　　いいえ、すきではありません。
Yes, I do like it.　　　No, I don't like it.

If you want to ask what someone's favorite sport is, ask:

Dono supōtsu ga ichiban suki desu ka?
どのスポーツが　いちばんすきですか。

Gorufu desu.
ゴルフです。
It's golf.

▢ With a partner.
　 Ask your partner which of these **supōtsu** he or she likes:
　 a swimming
　 b football
　 c basketball
　 d badminton

Behind the mask

Gekijō

Traditional theater is performed in a building called a **gekijō**. **Nō** (sometimes written as **noh**) is a type of theater that originated from singing and dancing at religious shrines.

About two hundred **nō** plays are still performed. Many of the stories have tragic themes, such as madness and the relationship between humans and gods. To balance the serious mood, there are **kyōgen**, lighthearted intervals with comic sketches, usually performed without masks.

Nō plays are performed only by men. The actors wear masks and have a whole range of subtle gestures and movements which makes nō acting seem slow-moving to people who do not know the traditions. ▶

能楽

文楽

◀ *Bunraku is puppet theater which dates back to the 16th century. The puppets are about two-thirds human size. Up to three puppeteers may be manipulating the actions of one main character. The puppeteers dress in black so that they blend into the background. Bunraku stories are about love, feuds and revenge.*

Kabuki is the most popular form of Japanese traditional theater. The plays include music and dance, and many of the stories are borrowed from **bunraku**.

As in **nō**, men take all the parts. The **onnagata**, the main female character, is one of the most famous and difficult roles in **kabuki**.

Other unique features of **kabuki** are a revolving stage which makes scene changes easier and the **hanamichi**, an extension of the stage which leads through the audience.

Kabuki actors speak in a stylized way, so even Japanese people make use of the earphones giving a simultaneous commentary in Japanese which are available at the Kabukiza (Kabuki Theater) in Tōkyō. ▶

歌舞伎

Shumi

Here are some traditional **shumi** (pastimes):

茶の湯

Chanoyu (The tea ceremony) is much more than making tea. **O cha** (tea) was introduced from China in the 8th century, but it was not until 400 years later that the Buddhist monks of the Zen sect began to develop the art of serving tea.

Nowadays, **chanoyu** is more of a social occasion, although the calm, ceremonial atmosphere and subtle movements are still important.

生花

Even though **ikebana**, or Japanese flower arranging, may look simple, there are careful rules for making these arrangements of twigs, leaves or flowers. Often **ikebana** is arranged to represent **ten**, **chi**, **jin** (heaven, earth and humankind).

Ikebana has a history in Japan going back over a thousand years. There are over 20 different schools of **ikebana** that each have their own style. **Sōgetsuryū** is one well-known style.

盆栽

Bonsai literally means 'tray plants'. They are trees which grow only about 50 cms (20 inches) high because the soil and water is limited to the minimum necessary for growth. Different trees are grown, including pine, cypress, plum and bamboo trees.

With patience and skill, the branches are grown into a shape that is considered artistic. Some **bonsai** are kept in families for up to 100 years.

折紙

Origami literally means 'folding' (**oru**) 'paper' (**kami**). Paper of different colors is folded to make shapes such as **asagao** (a morning glory flower) or **yakko-san** (a figure of a man).

Tsuru (above) are cranes, which symbolize long life and good fortune and are considered the most elegant example of **origami**. **Senbazuru**, a thousand small **tsuru** on a string, are given to someone who is ill, or to a sports team for good luck.

Dressing up

Kimono

The word **kimono** literally means 'clothes', but when people hear it most of them think of the traditional robe. Japanese men and women only wear **kimono** for special occasions. Men and boys wear **kimono** less often than women. Their **kimono** are made of wool and dyed blue or dark brown. At **O shōgatsu** (New Year), men sometimes wear a **kimono** to receive guests at home.

Girls and women wear **kimono** at coming-of-age and graduation ceremonies, wedding receptions, funeral services and for visiting shrines during **O shōgatsu**. Many women have three or more **kimono**, including longer-sleeved ones for formal occasions.

Young women wear brightly coloured **kimono** with flower or bird designs. The most ornate ones are made of silk and embroidered with silver and gold thread. Older women prefer darker shades and more subdued patterns.

A **montsuki** is a **kimono** with a **mon** (family crest) dyed on the front, back and sleeves. The most famous **mon** is the one for the emperor's family. It is a chrysanthemum with 16 petals.

*Couples often wear **kimono** at a wedding. The bride wears a special **uchikake kimono**, usually worn just once. It takes a lot of practice to put on and wear a **kimono** properly. Help is needed with the different layers, as well as the **obi**, the embroidered sash which goes round the waist.*

*A **yukata** is an unlined **kimono** made of cotton. It is comfortable for relaxing in at home during hot summer evenings. People also wear **yukata** outdoors at local festivals and hot-spring resorts. **Yukata** are always wrapped left over right and the belt is tied at the front.*

*Geta (wooden clogs) are worn with summer **kimono** and **yukata**. **Zōri** (right above) are for formal wear with **kimono**. Both **geta** and **zōri** have a V-shaped strap at the front. Special split-toed socks called **tabi** are worn with **geta** and **zōri**.*

Shigoto gi

Deciding about **shigoto gi**, or what to wear to work, is not difficult for Japanese workers. Even **sarariiman** (male company employees) have a kind of uniform: they all wear a **sūtsu** (a suit), a **shatsu** (a shirt) and a **nekutai** (a tie).

*As well as people who work in restaurant chains, **depāto** (department stores) and factories, **kaisha-in** (employees) working for larger companies usually wear a uniform at the office.*

Taxi drivers, elevator operators and some other workers wear white gloves. Although this may not seem very practical for some jobs, Japanese people consider that the right image is as important as practicality.

日本語

When you are shopping for clothes and **kutsu** (shoes), these phrases may be useful.

Kore o kite mite ii desu ka?
これをきてみていいですか。
Is it okay if I try this on?

Dō desu ka?
どうですか。
How is it?/How are they?

Chōdo ii desu.
ちょうどいいです。
It's a good fit./They're a good fit.

Ōki sugimasu.
おおきすぎます。
It's too big./They're too big.

Chiisa sugimasu.
ちいさすぎます。
It's too small./They're too small.

1 What answers in Japanese would these customers give to the shop assistant?
a The girl trying the T-shirt?
b The boy trying the belt?

The East

Tōkyō 東京

Although **Tōkyō** was largely rebuilt after a major earthquake in 1923 and heavy bombing in World War II, the opportunity for planned development was not taken. Many areas of this crowded modern city follow a random street pattern.

Also a port, **Tōkyō** is the heart of Japan and one of the world's most exciting and safest capitals.

*Near **Tōkyō Eki** (**Tōkyō** Station) is the **Marunouchi** district.* *is the main business area. From there, it is a short walk to the Imperial Palace, official residence of the emperor and his family (above). The main garden is open twice a year—on January 2 and December 23, the emperor's birthday—when the royal family waves to the crowds of well-wishers.*

*South of **Marunouchi** is **Ginza**, one of the main shopping areas. It is closed to traffic on Sundays (and national holidays) when Japanese families wander around the big **depāto** (department stores) and hi-tech showrooms. The most exclusive restaurants and nightclubs are also in this area.*

*An hour's train journey west of **Tōkyō** is **Hakone** which is full of mountain views including Japan's sacred (and highest) mountain, **Fuji-san**. There is also **Ashinoko** (Lake **Ashi**) and hot-spring resorts*

*In **Tōkyō**, **Fuji-san** can be glimpsed from the top of Sunshine 60, Japan's highest skyscraper, located in **Ikebukuro**, another district of fashionable stores which has a new arts center.*

◀ *In western **Tōkyō** is **Shinjuku** which has a cluster of skyscrapers and the new City Hall. The National Diet (Parliament) building and the Prime Minister's residence are in **Nagatachō**, about midway between **Shinjuku** and **Marunouchi**.*

***Shinjuku Eki** is the busiest station in Japan with an average of two million passengers passing through daily. **Shinjuku** and **Tōkyō Eki** are the capital's two largest stations.*

Kantō

Here are some other famous places in the Kantō region outside Tōkyō:

A view of Yokohama ▶ port

Out along **Tōkyō** Bay is **Yokohama**. Now Japan's busiest port, it was a quiet fishing village until 1854 when the Americans landed here.

Yokohama is also the second largest city in Japan, although it is usually included in the urban development known as **Keihin** which takes in **Kawasaki** and **Tōkyō** (about 30 minutes away).

In the center is **Chūkagai**, Japan's largest 'Chinatown' with about 150 Chinese restaurants. In **Yamate-machi**, some of the large houses built by wealthy western traders in the 19th century can still be seen.

The Tōkyō Tawā (Tōkyō Tower) is a familiar landmark in the city. Nearby is Roppongi, a popular entertainment area with discotheques and restaurants.

The Daibutsu (Great Buddha) is in the ▶ grounds of Kōtokuin Temple. It was cast in bronze in 1252 and is over 11 meters (36 feet) high. The inside is hollow and a staircase leads up to shoulder level.

Kamakura attracts many visitors who come to see the **Daibutsu**, or to enjoy the sandy beaches along **Sagami** Bay. The resort of **Katase** is popular with people from **Tōkyō** and is very crowded in the summer. Many writers and artists live in **Kamakura**.

For about 140 years from 1192, **Kamakura** was the capital of Japan. There are 65 Buddhist temples and 19 Shinto shrines, most of which date from that time.

Asakusa, in eastern Tōkyō, is in the area known as shitamachi (downtown). An old part of Tōkyō, Asakusa has one of the city's main tourist attractions: Sensōji or the Kannon Temple.

In the same area is spacious Ueno Kōen (Ueno Park) with museums and a fine concert hall in the grounds. In April the park is crowded with picnickers who come to view the sakura (cherry blossom).

◀ The bright colors and elaborate carvings of the Tōshōgu Shrine at Nikkō suggest some Chinese or Korean influence.

Set in a forest of Japanese cedars, the shrine complex at **Nikkō** has breathtaking mountain scenery and splendid religious buildings.

Just past the red **Shinkyō** (Sacred Bridge) and the **Rinnōji** Temple is the famous **Tōshōgū** Shrine, built in memory of **Ieyasu Tokugawa**, the first **shōgun** of the **Tokugawa** line. Started in 1636, it took 20 years to complete. Thousands of the best craftsmen were employed in the construction of the shrine and the other sacred 22 buildings (both Shinto and Buddhist).

The West

Ōsaka 大阪

Ōsaka is Japan's second city. Its central position on Japan's main island, **Honshū**, has made it a natural focus for trade over the centuries. From the 16th to the 19th century, it was the main commercial center for Japan. Traditionally known as 'the city of bridges' because of its 1,000 bridges, **Ōsaka** is better known now as a center for heavy industries that include shipyards, steel mills and car factories. Ten million people work in **Hanshin**, the urban industrial belt stretching from **Ōsaka to Kōbe** which also includes **Kyōto**.

*After the 1970 World Fair and the success of the more recent **Hanahaku** (Flower Festival) in 1990, the city authorities are keen to promote **Ōsaka** as an international city of the future.*
▼

*Ōsaka Jō (Ōsaka Castle) may look old, but it is a modern reconstruction built in 1931. The original castle on the site was completed in 1586 and was the largest in Japan. It was built for the **shōgun Toyotomi Hideyoshi**.*

Kōbe 神戸

Although **Kōbe** had already been a sizeable port for 600 years, it wasn't until foreign trade started to flourish in the mid-19th century that it became one of Japan's biggest seaports. Ocean-going passenger liners dock either in **Kōbe** or **Yokohama**.

The city of **Kōbe** is built on the narrow strip of land between **Seto Naikai** (the Inland Sea) and the **Rokkō-san** (Mount Rokkō) range. The main business and shopping areas, **Motomachi** and **Sannomiya**, are near the harbor. The residential areas are built on the lower hills that lead up to **Rokkō-san**.

*Cattle are reared in this area to provide **Kōbe** beef. It is said that the cattle are fed with beer and massaged to produce meat of the highest quality. The meat is, not surprisingly, very expensive.*

Kyōto 京都

Until 1868, **Kyōto** had been the capital of Japan for over a thousand years. It has about 1,500 temples in all, including many of the finest temples and gardens in Japan. Unlike **Ōsaka** and other major cities, **Kyōto** escaped the devastation of World War II because it was considered a treasure house of Japanese art.

Festivals are held in **Kyōto** throughout the year. One of the biggest is the **Gion Matsuri** (the **Gion** Festival) in July. There is a parade of floats, **samurai** and lion dancers.

At **Nijō Jō** (**Nijō** Castle), evidence of the lavish lifestyle of the **shōgun Ieyasu Tokugawa** can be seen. Famous gardens include the enigmatic Zen garden of 15 rocks and white sand at **Ryōanji** and the landscaped garden at the **Heian** Shrine. The spirit of ancient Japan manages to survive the 10 million visitors the city attracts every year.

*One of the best views of the city is from the terrace of **Kiyomizu-dera** (**Kiyomizu** Temple), a temple that was founded 1,200 years ago.*

◀ *A stroll along **Tetsu-gaku no michi** (Philosophers' Way) leads to the temple of **Ginkakuji** ('Silver Pavilion').*

*Biwa-ko (Lake **Biwa**), Japan's largest lake, is near **Kyōto**. It takes its name from the word for a lute because it has a similar shape.*

Nara 奈良

Situated 42 kilometers (26 miles) south of **Kyōto**, **Nara** was Japan's first permanent capital from 710 to 784. This **Nara** period was of importance because Buddhism had recently arrived from China. A strong Chinese influence is reflected in the art treasures from that time which are housed at the National Museum.

Temples, pagodas and shrines are dotted about **Nara Kōen** (**Nara** Park). **Kōfukuji** has a five-story pagoda dating from 1426. A large **torii** (sacred gate) leads the way to the **Kasuga** Shrine. It has 3,000 large stone and bronze lanterns that are lit twice a year: once for **Setsubun** in February and again in August.

*Sacred **shika** (deer) roam in **Nara Kōen**.*

*Inside **Tōdaiji** Temple you can see **Daibutsu** (the Great Buddha) which is the largest Buddha cast in bronze. The 15-meter- (50-feet-) statue is over 1,200 years old and various parts of it have been damaged and repaired over the years. The eyes are more than a meter (three feet) wide.*

The South

Shikoku 四国

Across **Seto Naikai** (the Inland Sea) from **Honshū** is the peaceful island of **Shikoku**. Its name means 'four provinces' and comes from the fact that it is divided into four **ken** (prefectures): **Tokushima**, **Kagawa**, **Kōchi** and **Ehime**. **Shikoku's** larger towns are situated on the coast, with mountains and rugged countryside inland. The coastline between Cape **Ashizuri** and **Uwajima** in the southwest is some of the most unspoilt in Japan.

Industries such as paper-making and pharmaceuticals flourish in the north-eastern town of **Takamatsu**. It also contains the **Ritsurin Kōen** (**Ritsurin** Park), a landscaped garden which spreads over 78 hectares (200 acres), dotted with lakes, rocks and tea houses. It took more than a hundred years to complete.

Kōchi, a farming and fishing center in the south of **Shikoku**, has a 17th-century castle and a traditional Sunday open-air market.

In **Tokushima-ken**, *terraces for growing rice and* ▶ *other crops are built up the mountainside.*

Every year, approximately 100,000 people come to **Shikoku** *to make a tour of the island's 88 sacred temples. The traditional pilgrimage is on foot and takes two months. Many modern pilgrims go round in two weeks by bus.*

The pilgrimage is in memory of the 8th-century Buddhist saint, **Kūkai**, *also known as* **Kōbō Daishi**, *who was born on the island. His teachings helped spread Buddhism through Japan.*

Ⓐ Look at the **kanji** (characters) that make up the word **Shikoku**. Find and write out the **kanji** for 'four.' (See pages 20–21.)

1️⃣ Which island on page 73 has a number nine in its name?

Hiroshima 広島

On August 6, 1945, the first atomic bomb was dropped on **Hiroshima** in southern **Honshū**. Up to 200,000 people died, more than half the population. As a reminder, the Atom Bomb Dome has been left. It is a ruined building that marks the epicenter of the atomic blast. The Peace Memorial Museum has dramatic displays of the terrible event and its aftermath.

The rebuilt city of **Hiroshima** is now the region's main industrial center, with industries such as shipbuilding, car manufacturing and petrochemicals. Its present population stands at around one million.

◀ *The Atom Bomb Dome in the Peace Memorial Park*

Miyajima 宮島

Just a short train and ferry ride from **Hiroshima** is **Miyajima**, an island with a long religious tradition. Japanese people consider that it offers one of the best views in the country.

Off the coast is a large red **torii** (sacred gate) which is part of the **Itsukushima** Shrine, founded in 592. There is a colorful festival in June, and performances of Japanese classical music are given at the shrine from time to time.

Deer and monkeys inhabit the island of **Miyajima**. A cable car goes up to the highest point on **Misen-san** (Mount **Misen**) from which there is a fine view across **Hiroshima** Bay.

*The **torii** and the shrine at **Miyajima** are built so that at high tide there is an impression that they are floating in the water.*

Kyūshū 九州

Because of its proximity to mainland Asia, **Kyūshū** has served as a gateway for foreign culture since olden times. A strong Chinese influence can be felt in **Nagasaki**, which was the only port that remained open to ships from abroad between the 16th to the 19th centuries. There was regular trade with Portugal, Spain and Holland. European ships also handled Japan's trade with China and the Philippines. **Nagasaki** also played a key role in the bringing of western knowledge and Christianity to Japan. (See pages 18–19.)

During World War II, **Nagasaki's** importance as a shipbuilding town made it the target of the second atomic bomb, three days after the first was dropped on **Hiroshima**. **Nagasaki** is still a leading port.

*In the old castle town of **Kumamoto** is **Suizenji Kōen** (**Suizenji** Park) which was laid out in 1632 for the powerful **Hosokawa** clan. This landscaped garden is noted for the brilliant miniature reproductions of Japanese beauty spots such as Mount **Fuji** and Lake **Biwa**.*

*On the east coast is the spa town of **Beppu**. It is no ordinary spa town for it has 3,000 hot springs. You can even have a **sunayu**, a bath in hot black sand! In some of the mud pools, known as **jigoku** (hell), scarlet-colored water bubbles up and mud is pushed violently into the air.*

*Almost in the center of **Kyūshū** is the world's largest volcanic crater, **Aso-san** (Mount **Aso**). Many myths concerning the founding of Japan are associated with this region. **Miyazaki**, a city in the southeast, contains a shrine dedicated to the legendary **Jimmu**, the first emperor.*

The North

Sendai 仙台

Sendai

Sendai, the principal town of the mountainous **Tōhoku** region, is located in **Miyagi ken** (**Miyagi** prefecture). It is a modern city, with wide tree-lined streets and many parks. **Sendai** was heavily bombed during World War II and many historical buildings were destroyed.

During the **Tokugawa** shogunate (1603–1867), the area around **Sendai** was under the control of the **Date** clan. In 1602, **Date Masamune** built **Aoba Jō** ('Green Leaf' Castle). Now only the remains of the castle ramparts are left.

*Twenty kilometers (12 miles) east of **Sendai** is **Matsushima** Bay which has hundreds of small islands and rocks covered with strangely-shaped pine trees. Like **Miyajima**, **Matsushima** is considered one of Japan's most scenic locations. A boat trip around the islands is perhaps the best way to enjoy **Matsushima**.*

Hokkaidō 北海道

Japan's second largest island, **Hokkaidō**, is noted for its wide open spaces and spectacular mountain scenery. The northernmost point of the island is Cape **Sōya** which is appropriately windswept and bleak. Fewer than 6,000,000 people live on this island which makes up more than 20 percent of Japan's land area.

Hokkaidō was given its present name at the start of the **Meiji** era (1868–1912). Its former name was *Ezo*. Until 1869, the island was inhabited mainly by the Ainu people and other tribes who had lived there for more than 1,000 years. Their simple way of life was changed as the **Yamato** Japanese from **Honshū** began to develop **Hokkaidō**.

***Shōwa Shinzan** is a reminder that Japan is a land of volcanoes. It is Japan's newest volcano. In July 1945, it began to rise slowly out of the ground. After seven months, it erupted to form a peak 400 meters (1,312 feet) high.*

*Northern **Hokkaidō** is one of Japan's most important farming areas. Crops include potatoes, sugar beet, soybeans and rice. Unlike other parts of Japan, the land is suitable for grazing cattle. The large number of cows produce milk which is turned into butter and other dairy products.*

Most of the Ainu have now integrated into mainstream society and have adopted Japanese names. About 20,000, including the Ainu chief above, try to preserve something of their culture by living in traditional villages.

Many place names in **Hokkaidō** are of **Ainu** origin, so sometimes it is difficult for visitors from other parts of Japan to pronounce them correctly.

Sapporo, the capital, is a relatively new city, dating from 1869. The grid-style layout of the capital was planned by an American and the avenues are numbered like streets in American cities.

Visitors flock here in February for **Yuki Matsuri** (the Snow Festival) before heading off to the ski slopes. The **matsuri** has huge ice sculptures of animals, legendary characters, and even buildings.

◀ These **tsuru** (cranes) are in the **Akan** National Park in the east of the island. In the park there are three lakes. **Kussharo-ko** is the largest. **Akan-ko**, located in a volcanic crater, has a famous and rare aquatic weed called **marimo**. **Mashū-ko** ('Devil's Lake') seems mysterious because mist often hangs over the water.

———— 日本語 ————

Look at the name **Hokkaidō** written in **kanji** (characters) on page 74. The first **kanji** means 'north'. It is pronounced **kita** and sometimes **hoku** when it is combined with other **kanji**.

北
Kita

西 ←——→ 東
Nishi   **Higashi**

南
Minami

The fishing port of **Hakodate** was opened to foreign trade in 1859. The western-style buildings in **Motomachi** near the port and the old-fashioned, wooden streetcars are reminders of that time.

The **Hakodate Hakubutsukan** is a museum for those interested in the history of **Hokkaidō**. It includes the story of the early tribes.

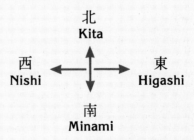

1   Carefully study the **kanji** for north, south, east and west. The **kanji** for 'east' appears in the name of a city on pages 68–69. Which city is it?

2   Now you should be able to say how the **kanji** for 'east' is pronounced when it is combined with another **kanji**?

Contrasts

Japan and the outside world

To avoid any possible acts of aggression by Japan in the solving of international problems, the new constitution after World War II renounced war. The country does, however, have a self-defense force about 250,000 strong. There are also 50,000 American troops stationed at bases throughout the country. Although the defense budget has traditionally been limited to about one percent of the gross national product, this is a considerable amount of money because Japan is such a rich country.

Japan's large trade surplus with other countries sometimes leads to strained relations with other countries. Other countries say that the complicated distribution system makes selling goods in Japan difficult. Japanese people say that perhaps foreign companies do not always understand the local way of doing business or make their goods appeal to Japanese customers.

Recently, Japan has tried to improve its relations with the countries nearest to it. Relations with China improved in the 1970s. A visit in 1989 by the South Korean president (above) and a review of the Japanese law that requires residents of Korean descent to carry identity cards may help to bring closer contacts with Japan's former colony.

The self-defense force on parade. During the Gulf ▶ crisis from 1990–91, the Japanese government faced a difficult situation when the United States questioned whether Japan, highly dependent on oil from the Middle East, should not send some auxiliary forces to Saudi Arabia. The Japanese took the option of offering a financial contribution towards the upkeep of the allied multi-national force in the Gulf.

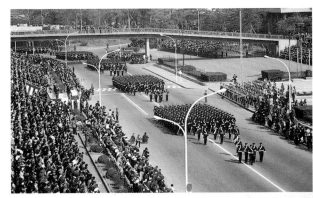

◀ *Although they come from a country that was closed off for so long, Japanese citizens and people of Japanese descent now live all over the world. Japanese immigrants have made new lives for themselves in North and South America. Alberto Fujimori, born of Japanese parents, recently became President of Peru.*

This is the Japanese area of Sao Paolo in Brazil. 550,000 Brazilians are of Japanese origin.

A foreign car is a status symbol. ▶ Clothes and food items from abroad are also fashionable because they are foreign.

The Japanese and nature

Many people in Japan consider that they have a 'special relationship' with nature. The countryside of Japan—the mountains, lakes and streams—has provided inspiration for countless artists and writers.

This 'special relationship' does not always work both ways. People appreciate the beauty of a natural scene, but **Fuji-san** (Mount **Fuji**) is strewn with the litter left by those climbing this sacred mountain. Advertising boards in fields intrude into country settings. At some places, loudspeakers giving information or playing loud music are unwelcome distractions.

The fiery colors of autumn leaves and spring-time **sakura** (cherry blossom) have a special place in the hearts of the Japanese.

A short trip down the peaceful **Katsura** river is interrupted for a quick snack.

Since most people live in towns, they like to keep in ▶ touch with nature through seasonal decorations. They put spring or autumn wallhangings up in their homes. Shopkeepers also decorate their shops. In this **Kyōto** street there are sprays of plastic autumn leaves.

◀ Japan has been criticized for whaling and for its huge imports of timber to satisfy the nation's demands for excessive packaging and items such as disposable wooden chopsticks for restaurants.

The growing international concern for environmental issues is making more Japanese people aware that their country will have to play its part. As a small gesture, some people have started taking their own reusable chopsticks to restaurants.

Hiragana

あ	a	い	i	う	u	え	e	お	o
か	ka	き	ki	く	ku	け	ke	こ	ko
が	ga	ぎ	gi	ぐ	gu	げ	ge	ご	go
さ	sa	し	shi	す	su	せ	se	そ	so
ざ	za	じ	ji	ず	zu	ぜ	ze	ぞ	zo
た	ta	ち	chi	つ	tsu	て	te	と	to
だ	da	(ぢ)	(ji)	(づ)	(zu)	で	de	ど	do
な	na	に	ni	ぬ	nu	ね	ne	の	no
は	ha	ひ	hi	ふ	fu	へ	he	ほ	ho
ば	ba	び	bi	ぶ	bu	べ	be	ぼ	bo
ぱ	pa	ぴ	pi	ぷ	pu	ぺ	pe	ぽ	po
ま	ma	み	mi	む	mu	め	me	も	mo
や	ya			ゆ	yu			よ	yo
ら	ra	り	ri	る	ru	れ	re	ろ	ro
わ	wa								
ん	n								

- See how the sounds of *k, s,* ｜ and *h* are changed by adding special marks ゛ (**dakuten**). Example:
  ごはん **gohan** (rice, meal)
  ざぶとん **zabuton** (cushion)
  Han dakuten ゜ changes *h* into a *p* sound.

- A long vowel is written by adding the sign for the vowel, i.e. *a, i, u* or *e*. A long *o* is written using the **hiragana** for *u*.
  For example:
  おばあさん **obāsan** (grandmother)
  ありがとう **arigatō** (thank you)

- A small **tsu** before a consonant is not pronounced but it doubles the consonant which follows it.
  Example:
  けっこう **kekkō** (all right)

- **Hiragana** can be combined with *ya, i, yu, e* or *yo* to form another syllable which includes a *y* sound. The second **hiragana** is written smaller.
  Example:
  きゅう **kyū** (nine, 9)
  ちゅうしょく **chūshoku** (lunch｜
  しょうぐん **shōgun**
  とうきょう **Tōkyō**

Particles
There are words called particles which occur often in Japanese. The following particles are written:
は **wa**   を **o**   へ **e**
Example:
Yukio wa kōhii o nomimasu.
ゆきおはコーヒーをのみます。
Yukio drinks coffee.

Kono basu wa Tōkyō eki e ikimasu.
このバスはとうきょうえきへ
いきます。
This bus goes to **Tōkyō** Station.

Katakana

ア	a	イ	i	ウ	u	エ	e	オ	o
カ	ka	キ	ki	ク	ku	ケ	ke	コ	ko
ガ	ga	ギ	gi	グ	gu	ゲ	ge	ゴ	go
サ	sa	シ	shi	ス	su	セ	se	ソ	so
ザ	za	ジ	ji	ズ	zu	ゼ	ze	ゾ	zo
タ	ta	チ	chi	ツ	tsu	テ	te	ト	to
ダ	da	(ヂ)	(ji)	(ヅ)	(zu)	デ	de	ド	do
ナ	na	ニ	ni	ヌ	nu	ネ	ne	ノ	no
ハ	ha	ヒ	hi	フ	fu	ヘ	he	ホ	ho
バ	ba	ビ	bi	ブ	bu	ベ	be	ボ	bo
パ	pa	ピ	pi	プ	pu	ペ	pe	ポ	po
マ	ma	ミ	mi	ム	mu	メ	me	モ	mo
ヤ	ya			ユ	yu			ヨ	yo
ラ	ra	リ	ri	ル	ru	レ	re	ロ	ro
ワ	wa								
ン	n								

- See how the sounds of *k*, *s*, *t* and *h* are changed by adding special marks ゛(**dakuten**). **Han dakuten** ゜ changes *h* into a *p* sound.
Example:
ハンバーガー **hanbāgā** (hamburger)
パン **pan** (bread)

- A long vowel sound is shown by adding — after the **katakana**. This doubles the length of the vowel.
Example:
コーヒー **kōhii** (coffee)
デパート **depāto** (department store)

- A small **tsu** before a consonant is not pronounced but it doubles the consonant which follows it.
Example:
ホットドッグ **hotto doggu** (hot-dog)

- **Katakana** can be combined with *ya, i, yu, e* or *yo* to form another syllable which includes a *y* sound. The second **katakana** is written smaller.
Example:
ジュース **jūsu** (juice)
ニュージーランド **Nyū Jiirando** (New Zealand)
シャワー **shawā** (shower)

- When writing foreign words beginning with *f*, use **fu** followed by the vowel written smaller beside it:
Example:
ファ **fa**, フィ **fi**, フェ **fe**, フォ **fo**, フォーク **fōku** (fork).

Answers

Page 7: ☐ **a** fried chicken, **b** juice, **c** chocolate, **d** baby carriage, **e** laundromat, **f** department store, **g** mansion (apartment block).

Page 8: 1 A Katsuhiro, B Yoshie. **2 a** Dōmo arigatō, **b** Ohayō gozaimasu, **c** Nihongo ga hanasemasu ka? **3 a** Thank you, **b** Good morning, **c** Can you speak Japanese? **4 a** Mel Gibson (**Meru Gibuson**), **b** Madonna, **c** George Bush (**Jyōji Busshyu**), **d** Mikhail Gorbachev (**Mihairu Gorubachofu**).

Page 11: 1 a Sumimasen. **b** O yasuminasai. **c** Anata no namae wa? **d** Hajimemashite. **e** . . . desu, **f** Jā ne.

Page 20: 1 a ni-jū-roku 二十六. **b** yon-jū-nana 四十七. **c** go-jū-kyū 五十九. **d** san-jū-san 三十三. **e** hachi-jū-go 八十五. **Page 21:** September 2, 1991.

Page 23: 1 b California University Berkeley (**Kariforunia Daigaku Bākurei**), **b** Sydney University (**Shidonii Daigaku**). **2** Ice cream (**Aisu kuriimu o ikaga desu ka?**)

Page 24: ☐ **a** shichi-ji juppun, **b** ni-ji san-jū-roppun, **c** hachi-ji gofun, **d** jū-ichi-ji jū-nifun, **e** jū-ji, **f** jū-ni-ji juppun, **g** jū-ni-ji yon-jū-hachi fun.

Page 28: 1 Tom Cruise (**Tomu Kurūzu**), Days of Thunder (**Deizu obu sandā**). **Page 29: 2** N. **3** Two weather bulletins at 6.45 (after the news) and 7 p.m. **4 a** リビングナウ. **b** クイズ. **c** フランス. **d** セサミストリート. **e** ニュース. **f** オンステージ.

5 a 6 p.m. Channel 3, **b** 7.20 p.m. Channel 1, **c** 4.05 p.m. Channel 1, **d** 5 p.m. Channel 3, **e** 5 p.m., 6.45 pm & 7pm Channel 1, **f** 5.05 p.m. Channel 1.

Page 37: Dōmo arigatō.

Page 38: 1 Ozawa Seiji, Uchida Mitsuko, Morita Akio, Mori Hanae もりはなえ, Miyake Issey みやけいっせい, Takada Kenzō. Note: **Tamori** is always written in **katakana**.

Page 41: 1 Paruko パルコ, Exit 6.

Page 43: 1 1,516 千五百十六, 8,951 八千九百五十一, 9,999 九千九百九十九. **a** ni-sen san-byaku yon-jū-go, **b** kyū-sen happyaku shichi-jū-roku, **c** roppyaku san, **d** yon-sen nana-hyaku jū-ichi, **e** san-zen roppyaku roku-jū-shichi, **f** sen hachi-jū-hachi, **g** nana-sen ni-hyaku, **h** go-hyaku kyū-jū-kyū.

Page 44: 1 Left. **Page 45: 2** getsuyōbi (**Monday**), suiyōbi (Wednesday), kinyōbi (Friday). **3** Tamagawa Gakuen. **4** 8 chōme. **5 a** 5 chōme, **b** 3 chōme.

Page 47: 1 a 1st floor, **b** 4th floor, **c** 3rd floor.

Page 49: ☐ **a** ni-man hassen kyū hyaku hachi-jū-san 二万八千九百八十三. **b** jū-kyū-man ni-sen hyaku jū-nana 十九万二千百十七. **c** go-jū-roku-man nana-sen hyaku 五十六万七千百. **d** ichi-man kyū-jū-kyū 一万九千九十九. **e** hyaku-man nana-hyaku hachi-jū-kyū 百万七百八十九. **f** roku-man roku-sen yon-hyaku yon-jū-ni 六万六千四百四十二. **g** hachi-man nana-sen hyaku yon 八万七千百四, **h** ni-hyaku-yon-jū-roku-man nana-sen kyū-hyaku ni-jū-ichi 二百四十六万七千九百二十一. **2 a** 100,00 yen, **b** 971,000 yen, **c** 8,500 yen.

Page 50: 1 Roku-ji ni shimarimasu

Page 51: 2 A fan. **3** No, he wants t pay less.

Page 55: 1 ハンバーガー. ☐ **a** chiizu bāgā (**cheeseburger**), **b** fisshyu bāgā (fishburger), **c** furaido poteto (French fries or frie potatoes), **d** kōhii (coffee), **e** orenj jūsu (orange juice), **f** banira sheik (vanilla milkshake). **2** c, teriyak bāgā, furaido poteto, guriin sarad **a** Fisshyu bāgā o mittsu kudasa **b** Hanbāgā o hitotsu to kōhii hitotsu kudasai. **c** Chiizu bāgā futatsu to banira sheiku o mitts kudasai. **d** Teriyaki bāgā o mutts to tako sarada o yottsu kudasai. Hanbāgā o yattsu to furaido potet o nanatsu kudasai.

Page 56: ☐ **a** Yon-jū-ichi en o kitte o go mai kudasai. **b** Roku-jū- en no kitte o kyū mai kudasa **c** Hyaku ni-jū en no kitte o roku ma kudasai. **d** Jū en no kitte o ni-jū kudasai. **Page 57: 1 a** Chotto matt kudasai. **b** Suzuki-san irasshai masu ka? **c** Moshi moshi. **d** Takan desu. **e** Hai, imasu.

Page 61: 1 a6, b2, c5, d3, e4, f1.

Page 67: 1 a Oki sugimasu. (It's to big). **b** Chiisa sugimasu. (It's to small.)

Page 72: Kyūshū.

Page 75: 1 Tōkyō ('Easter Capital'). **2** tō.

Photos

Front cover: Japan National Tourist Organization, London. **Back cover:** Japan National Tourist Organization, London; P. Hinder.
Asahi Shinbun 5; BFI Stills, Posters and Designs 39: Chancerel/P. Cassidy 15, 18, 22, 23, 31 (2), 33, 35 (3), 36, 49, 50, 51, 52, 59, 67, 70 (2), 77 (2); Chancerel/D. Prowse 4 (2), 9, 24 (2), 29, 34, 35 (3), 36, 42, 48, 49, 50 (2), 58, 59 (2), 60, 68 (2), 76; Fuji Sankei Communications Ltd. 39; Greenpeace Communications Ltd. 77; P. Hinder 4, 5, 6 (3), 7 (6), 8 (3), 9 (3), 10 (5), 11 (2), 12 (2), 14, 15 (2), 16, 19, 22 (2), 23 (3), 24 (3), 25 (6), 26, 27 (2), 28 (4), 29, 30 (2), 31 (2), 33, 34 (2), 35, 37 (6), 40 (6), 41 (3), 42, 44 (4), 45 (3), 46 (5), 47 (2), 48, 49 (2), 50, 51 (5), 52 (2), 54 (4), 55 (3), 56 (2), 57 (3), 58 (2), 59 (7), 60 (4), 61 (2), 63 (3), 65 (2), 66 (4), 67, 68 (3), 69; Japan Airlines 43; Japan Information Center, Japanese Embassy, London 20, 24, 60, 64, 77; Japan National Tourist Organization, London 11, 14, 15, 17, 18, 26, 30 (2), 32 (3), 33, 34, 45, 46, 47, 53 60, 62, 64 (2), 65 (3), 68, 69 (2), 70 (2), 71 (3), 72 (3), 7: (4), 74 (3), 75 (4), 77; Kenzo Paris/Peter Lindbergh 39 Thelma Krotoszynski 76; Kotobuki Corporation 27 Kyodo News Service 20 (2), 58, 63, 70, 76; Mansel Collection 17, 18, 19 (2), 20 (2); Nissan Europe N.V. 26, 27 Photo R.M.N. 16, 19; Steve J. Sherman 38; Sony (UK) Ltd 5, 38; J. Stock 15; M. Watson 48 (7).

Every effort has been made to contact the copyrigh holders of all illustrations. The publishers apologize fo any omissions and will be please to make the necessar arrangements at the first opportunity.

Acknowledgements

Boston Symphony Orchestra; Minako Furuta; Japan Rai Tokai; JTB, London; Chiyo Kusumoto; Staff and student of Shukutoku Gakuen and Seishin Tandai, Japan; JTB.